For Taylor Robinson, Ashley Craig, Brittany Marshall and Michelle Starkey.

For different reasons, Thanks.

"And there ain't shit

I would not not say

Or not not do nigga"

Eric Micheal Ward, Salty Niggas Preserve Everything. 2019

Part 1

Hi, I'm Adam.

Or

I think most days I'm a man on a deserted island who sees a rescue plane fly overhead but is too proud to jump up and shout, "help me, help me!" so instead he writes something esoteric with seashells in the sand and when planes fly overhead they don't stop to help because they don't get what "Free Smoke" means.

I can't begin to tell you how often I hate people for things they didn't actually do. A huge portion of my time is spent mulling over some perceived injustice I've endured or hypothesizing about potential transgressions brewing against me. I don't have just a few trust issues; I have the whole trust almanac. A collector's edition trust issue compendium. I'm afraid of everyone for things they might think or do. This leads me to shun and run from others and to hide my true essence for one of many personas. I'm sure you've met one and chances are he was underwhelming. I change persona's like Apple updates iOS, only I don't always get better, so maybe it's the exact same as iOS.

Ever since I can remember I've always had an aversion to healthy feelings of closeness or intimacy. When I feel it, true closeness, it's sort of the way a belt buckle can jab you in the gut when you're sitting down, not torturous pain, but sudden, sharp discomfort. Like the shell of a sunflower seed stuck in my teeth.

Do white people eat sunflower seeds? Is this relatable and accessible? I did a Google search for whether white people ate sunflower seeds and while I found no definitive answer, I did come across a website called 'stuffghettopeoplelike.com' that was updated frequently from 2008-2009 before stopping, and my new mission in life is to find the author of stuffghettopeplelike.com and encourage them to continue.

I'm writing this in the middle of a pandemic where the government is enforcing social distancing and isolation. But I've been social distancing for 30 years, just in rooms full of people.

The number one thing people say about my writing is that it is honest and vulnerable. And I resent that, it is not really a compliment, it is more of observation of how abominable my truth is. All that hiding, all that silent hating I do is only offset by the writing, its vulnerability and the fact that you read it. So thank you.

This story is about a lot of different things so I'll need you to keep up.

As a child I spent a lot of time alone.

 I grew up in a home with 3 old people whose primary interests were religious/political debates and covertly drinking whiskey. It wasn't until long that I saw the danger of this combination. Very rarely does one enter an argument about the existence of divinity with the willingness to have their mind changed. Especially on Saturday morning. So when these debates would occur I'd vanish like only an only child can. One of the perks of being an only child is the keen ability to sense when no one is watching you. To sense when the attention finally or regrettably, is no longer on you. It makes disappearing acts a natural feat. Most magicians are only children.

In those great stretches of time spent in willful isolation, I occupied myself with a lot of different things. Making Legos into castles, affecting mini-cruelties onto my cat. All of which were all paid back with claws and teeth. Felix always squared her debts.) And trying to figure out the right bend in the cord of the cable adapter that would remove the static and snow from the 15-inch TV in my room so that the Spice Channel was almost clear.

The Spice channel played a twenty-four hour loop of pay-per-view porn. Commercial free. One nudie flick after another, perennially. Sometimes, I'd spend what felt like gleeful eternities twisting the cable cord, hanging it on chair arms and weighing it down with Batman figures to find that perfect curvature that melted the army of epileptic digital ants away to reveal cartoonishly large boobs and explosions of teased, tall blonde hair. It was 1994 and media was still very much living in the neon fallout the 80's before Kurt Cobain had us all in oversized flannels and before Will Smith taught us to flip the brims of our caps the world was still rocking shoulder pads and leg warmers, and this was never more the case than with the women on the Spice Channel. That was before they undressed of course.

The week I was quarantined to my room with the chicken pox was particularly degenerative. I wasn't allowed to go to school and the only time my parents let me leave the confines of my carolina blue tinted bedroom was to relieve my bowels and bladder or bathe in oatmeal. (To this day whenever I see a package of Quaker Oats I look at the fellow in the Quaker garb thank him for helping me and my pox and also to all the Quakers for their role in abolishing slavery. Fistbump your local Quaker. Yes they still exist.) That week I spent my time with Super Mario and a silly string my father had purchased to cut through the boredom of being isolated. I appreciated the silly string, my father is notorious for thoughtful gifts of that nature, but I was hardly bored, I had the fuzzy silhouettes of hundreds of adults, rubbing one another, to keep me occupied.

It was a 6 year old's version of "Leaving Las Vegas."

Spice TV in the 90's was a far cry from the brash and brutal images depicted in today's porn. Spice TV seemed romantic in a way, but in a faint way, like the way dime store love novels, or Chris Isaak songs seem romantic. The way the camera would pan up exposed legs, the caressing of breasts, kissing the cheek of the butt; not tongue javelining the asshole that seems to be the industry standard of this golden year 2020. We live in an era of immediate and often ghoulish gratification, foreplay will die along with the boomers. It was soft and there was none of the brutish thrusts that I know sex to consist of now. It was almost like dancing among jellyfish, moving with an almost gelatinous quality over one another, like spreading jam on an English muffin.

It seemed sweetly carnal.

Seeing sex depicted on television felt like a feeble, ill-kept secret, or a forgotten lyric to a song you used to love. Seeing sex as a kid can be like going to place you've visited in a dream. It seemed foreign yet familiar, far off yet under the nose. Like screaming in a different language, the emotion is clear, but the specifics and details are hazy.

One of these details that was lost on me was that of the vagina.

Spice TV informed me that nudity was a requirement for sex. That was the first step; you had to be bare. And then there was kissing. I knew that heavy kissing was mandated. Maybe the woman would lift her leg and that leg would be grasped at the thigh by the man and this position seemed to be the pinnacle of passion to me. The woman suspended, like Jean Grey when she kissed Wolverine on the cover of Uncanny X-men issue 394. (Google it right now, that cover is Ian Churchill's seminal work.)

But Spice TV only played XX porn, and for a film to earn the third and final X it must depict penetration.

So the films lacked a key aspect, thus I lacked a formative understanding. Without shots of penetration, I didn't see vaginas. Without visual confirmation that vaginas even existed, I was forced to assume that all participating parties had my same equipment; a penis.

I see the male go down on the female. I see the back of his head; wiggling and writhing. I see the woman grasp the sheets, gyrating her pelvis. The camera would zoom in on her face, her eye; slits of white. Her teeth eating her own lips, cannibalizing herself. This feeling, I thought as a child, much too young and sheltered and dim in the ways that most children are dim, was so good that it would make you eat yourself.

This feeling, I know now, was clitoral stimulation. But at six, I thought they were sucking each other's dicks and drinking their pee.

I thought that when you were an adult, you found a beautiful woman. Through romantic acts like flowers and sailboat rides, you made her love you. When you were in love, the greatest gift you could give someone was sucking their dick and drinking their pee.

Because everyone had a dick, and what a relief it would be not to have to travel to the bathroom.

In my Catholic school polo and slacks, my hands so tiny and soft, I scanned the room of Ms. Sconier's second grade class. I'd look at the girls with pigtails and their necklaces that when combined with a friends necklace to spell out "best friends." Their Catholic school girl skirts exposing their knobby knees leading up to what I knew were penises, just like mine. I thought how if I could just get a girlfriend. Little, shy, eczema scared, stuttering me, could get a girlfriend, I'd treat her so good, open all the doors, share all my candy, and she'd have to let me drink her pee.

I knew I didn't want to drink any boy's piss, I wasn't attracted to boys. They had short hair and wore pants. I wanted the girls with the pig tails and the skirts.

 Once, Marissa Ellis and I sat in the back of an empty church. We were supposed to be gathering red pens from the supply closet to grade papers. But as the practice was, when the teacher sent you on an errand you took the longest possible route, and this route passed through the church that was attached to the school on the West end. We sat for a minute in a closed off vestibule with windows that looked on as candles on alters flicked underneath a porcelain Virgin Mary, looking on to the church, where both of us served as Alter Keepers, she looked at me, and in that strange, blunt, adventurous way children do, she lept in for a kiss. I'd never been kissed before, not by a woman who wasn't my mother but this kiss felt nothing like my mom's kiss. This kiss felt like she would have let me drink her pee.

From that day on, I abandoned my lunch table, where Everett and Justin and Kenan and James and Andrew pontificated battle scenarios between Digimon and Pokemon, for the girls section of the lunch room. And that is when I discovered, that through all my faults, my height and my wardrobe and my eczema (which had gotten so bad kids referred to me has spots or "He got what Michael Jackson got, don't make fun of him") I realized that I could occupy any seat, as long as I made people laughed when I got there. I'd sit among the girls and I was useful. I wasn't useful in dodge ball or on group projects, but at the lunch table, I had an arena, sold out shows every day, and fans who asked me to tell jokes again and again. If I was doing a character, they'd ask us the same voice again, they wanted the hits, they wanted encores. And there it hit me like a Randy Savage elbow drop; that this was how I'd drink their pee. If I kept them laughing, it was only a matter of time until that pee-pee would be mine.

I'd envision having all of them as my girlfriends, like the man had done in Harry Haram's, a Spice. They seemed happy together, and to a degree I was happy with them. I'd sit in the middle and they'd make space for me. I'd make them laugh, and look at their necks and their thin fingers and listen to their voices, their laughs sounded like perfectly modulated AMSR to me. Every night I'd retreat to my room and try and twist and turn the cord to present the clarity of my porn. I was consumed with pee-pee, there would be rumbles in my gut, that seemed to harken back to something ancient, something ceremonial, like a pagan ritual.

I must consume the pee-pee of all the girls in the land. Forever, until my stomach burst.

Obviously, I now know that the majority of women don't have penises. (I also realize genitalia doesn't and has never denoted gender.) Thus, I no longer have the urge to put penises in my mouth.

But this one time, at an airbnb in New York, a girl with eyes as blue as the ocean, well, nevermind.

The difference between 15 sexual partners and 30

(Might be something)

Imagine there was a device capable of telling you exactly how many sexual partners you'd have during the span of your life.

You'd power on the machine and it would travel through a wormhole and observe your life from the 5th dimension. From this precognitive state, it would count the number of unique sexual partners you had, then travel back through the wormhole with a number.

 Maybe the machine was given to you by a hyper-advanced alien civilization, or maybe it was a crystal given to you by some tree nymph. Or maybe the number appears in the smoke or in the dancing lashes of fire in a ritual you conduct over a pit with strange spices and ancient roots of long dead trees, and the bones of owls and the teeth of orphans.

With such capabilities one could prevent national tragedies, bring complex formulas for vaccines from the distant future to the here and now, and bet on every winner of horse and dog races. You could tell loved ones how much they meant before you couldn't anymore.

 But what if the device's only application was to display the exact number of sexual partners you'll have when you die. Would you be pissed?

What if the number that was displayed was 2,000, would you assume you finally made it big? You were a household name and with that notoriety came droves of suitors waiting for you to bed them. You were their brush with fame, you were their liaison with the immortals.

Or maybe you just went to Burning Man.

I have a friend that is a member of an orgy group that has monthly "meetings" at a condo in the Gold Coast. She says most of the members are very attractive and she wouldn't have a problem putting in a good word if I wanted to apply. Before the orgy is a cocktail hour where you talk to everyone at the party and if conversation goes well and attraction holds up, you exchange cards, and that is meant to be the green light for consensual orgy-based boning. What if I attend and no one gives me a card? Then I'm stuck on the outskirts of the orgy, sipping champagne and wondering why I'm even still naked?

What if the number was only two more than your current number? Would you assume that the person you are seeing now, despite whatever amount of time you've spent together, despite the fact you know her father on a first name basis, despite the fact you share a dog, or even more irresponsible, you share a fucking child, there would be two more lovers?

What if you love the person you're with so deeply that even the *thought* of attractive of nude bodies feels viscerally wrong, like eating apple pie while it's cold.

And it's only two more people, but why two, you'd think?

What happens after that second new body? Is that second body the body you'll be with? Or do you go back to one of the previous ones?

Or will you die, thus ending the stream of bodies. Maybe grief will take you. Grief took my aunt, and my grandfather, my Dad says it'll take him too.   Let's say the love of your life is your fifteenth sexual partner. Maybe your number fifteen died in a car wreck. Your sixteen and seventeen didn't come until years later. You kept text messages from fifteen, you kept number fifteen's shirts. You keep fifteen's memories stitched into your heart and soul so fundamentally that you become a patchwork of grief. You become a walking mausoleum.

I researched this and you won't fucking believe ir but I swear its true:

The average American has 7.256 sexual partners. This number seemed absurdly low to me at first. But, after considering the age of those surveyed, the multitude of caveats (religion, region, income, and preference), not to mention the ballistic rise of incel culture, I suppose 7.256 is a believable number.

Even though the .256 is weird, how do fuck .256th of a person?

Also, in the entire state of Utah the average is 2.6, which means we're all whores in Utah.

Which is, maybe the name of my new book.

What if you got your number back and it was double your current number.

So what if you're at fifteen and the machine tells you that when you die you'll be at thirty. Imagine all the life that transpired to get you to that fifteen. The heartbreak, the joy, the weird morning after and the conversations you'd hope would never end.

You'd maybe live double the life, but with more of grasp on shit than you did the first time. You could be better, more honest and more caring, and when things ran their course you could sit the person down and say, "I've been here before, it's best if I go that way and you go this way."

Because fifteen lovers a lot but thirty is life time more.

Ward off the ghosts

My friend, at the time of me writing this, is eight months into his new divorced life. He has a large black and white portrait that sits against the wall in his apartment, He and his ex-wife. They smile in this simple, happy way.Like the elation you get right after you kiss after an argument and your limbs feel light again. The elation you get after the tension breaks and your ears aren't so hot anymore. The elation you get after you fuck and you feel as pleasantly dull as a dog with its head out of window, tongue out, wind forcing open eyes to squinting slits.

They smile and even in the coolness of black and white I still feel the warmth. They seemed so happy.

He lived in the apartment after they got divorced. I can't imagine that when most people sign a lease with a spouse, their minds ever drift to whether the four walls will ever play setting to a break down.

"This is a nice place to stop fucking in, to resent in, to grow cold and distant and batter each other with words and glares and silence."

This is a nice place to realize this ain't it in.

I imagine I will now, part of me hopes you will too. Just maybe don't bring it up.

He keeps that picture close though, his ring is off, he writes mean poems about it, but the picture remains, because why shouldn't we have keepsakes of ancient beauty.

People stare at paintings of the Mona Lisa and her "beauty" (to me she resembles an actress for a Zantac commercial. Not to say unpretty, but to say why paint an actress in a Zantac commercial if it wasn't love.) and in reality, she's dust now.

I'd keep that picture too, I'd keep it because, no matter how it ended up, in that moment, that the photo was taken, I was happy. Between the flash and sky and God, I was happy. And maybe that's what matters.

Something

or

The day I considered getting a massage

An Uber driver and I held hands and prayed over my soul.

The tender nature of my soul, my tender soul that so often is outfitted with the fungal growth of this dirty world.

We held hands and he made me repeat after him:

"Say that Satan has no control over you."

"Satan has no control over me."

"Say you are in the service of what is just and right."

"I am…I am in service of what is just and right."

He, the Uber Driver, said he used to smoke crack for a time in his youth and he told me that he had done time and he had the twang in his voice of a man who didn't need to lie, and even scarier: who would tell the absolute truth at any given time.

To let in the love of the lord is difficult to me because it means so many foolish people are right about maybe the most important concept in all of existence.

We all wait for those moments, the ones that fundamentally change you for the better and I think we all foolishly think clarity comes in broad, massive bursts of awareness, clarity isn't always instant like gunshots. I think clarity more often creeps quietly, like a vine growing up in a house. Sporting lovely flowers, eventually.

Women stopped being bi-plane pilots when I turned 26. I need to make my own raft.

I knew a kid in middle school who would give girls a weekly stipend of five dollars so that they would tell the rest of the school they were his girlfriends. He deemed it a responsible allocation of his allowance to pay girls to publically fake a relationship. No kissing, or hand holding, maybe he'd call them on the phone and maybe out of some deep learned empathy the girls would answer and talk to him for a few minutes between homework and Neopets. I think at his height Carl had 3 girlfriends, a miniature harem. This sort of thing, polygamy, raises high brows now but at 11 and 12, it seemed infinitely simpler to grasp; that the heart often works outside the parameters of monogamy.

What I now find the most interesting was that he wasn't paying the girls who sat in the shade with us during recess reading video game manuals. Those girls were usually cross eyed, or wore their brother's hand me downs because 'he had already graduated and there is no need to buy new school pants.' Or something like that.

 He was paying the girls whose moms helped them flat ironed their hair every morning and who read Zane books during independent reading time. He paid the girls with the boyfriends in High School.

For a while we didn't know they were own his payroll, we just thought stuff like;

 'Oh Carl (Obviously not his name but to protect the innocent, Carl it is.) must just be great at talking to girls. Or maybe it's because he has his ear pierced.'

I forgot how the truth finally came out, maybe he missed a payment or the questions like 'why are you dating a lame?' got too much to handle for the girl. It wasn't long until the whole school knew Carl was paying for girlfriends. Naturally they all left and with his haram dissipated, Carl felt ashamed. He was back to reading Final Fantasy strategy guides in the shade with us. I guess the grief from his crumbled charade caused him to rediscover the value of defeating the Tonberry in Ipsen's Castle.

And I guess my central wonder is whether Carl ever did find a healthier way to get girls attention, or did he ever find the self-awareness and confidence to see the value of the girls in trenches with him, the ones in the shade with the cuffed pant legs.

But sometimes that seems impossible, sometimes it feels like everything men do is a desperate attempt to attract a woman. Desperate like flailing your arms at a biplane that passes the island you've been deserted on. You can't really pay a bi-plane pilot to rescue you. If the bi-plane pilot knows you have ample sources of fish and shelter they'll fly past you.

Landing a Bi-Plane is hard, especially on something so unstable like sand, especially for someone who hasn't showered and has been having sex with hollowed out coconuts with spit and mashed up slugs inside.

Immigration mandated Pheromones

When you come to America from like Saudi Arabia or another Middle East location, does the America consulate like, give all the men the same Burberry cologne? At the airport does someone say "Welcome to America. Here's a bottle of Burberry cologne make sure you go to clubs with 15 other Middle Eastern guys and you all wear it so it's less like you're 15 individual people and more so you like a sentient mist of Burberry named Anwar."

After this I only buy Balsamic.

Saw a woman eating a salad alone at the bar and I worked up the nerve to talk to her,

"What sort of dressing is that?"

"French. I got a salad because I'm boring."

"That's French dressing? Is French Dressing traditionally red?"

Her eyes narrow, and she gives me a look almost like she's looking through me. A look that successfully conveyed wonder, disappointment and pity.

"Yes" She answers. And gets so quiet I can hear the world turn.

That's right I asked a woman, nay I asked a HUMAN BEING, one that has experienced grief and love and rain after a goodbye and 9/11 and all sorts of other layered human experiences, Was French Dressing traditionally red? No words have EVER been arranged in such a lame way. How the fuck do you respond to 'Is French Dressing traditionally red? 'Why would you respond to such a dumb thing? No one has ever been telling a story to their friends about how they met their husband.

"And then he asked me what color French Dressing traditionally was. And that's how I knew he was the one. He's so smooth."

Sometimes I battle in my head over if it's me that's hard to talk to or the rest of the world? And French Dressing gate revealed that It's totally me. It's me because if I really like you, if I want to woo you, I'll ask you is French Dressing is traditionally red.

MAYA
Or
The rush of serotonin I get still, 8 years later when I ride past the Sheffield red line stop.

I just played pool by myself and it reminded me of this one time at Sheffield's when I played pool with this girl who was so far outta my league it may as well of been another sport.

I mean, I know I'm sort of cute but I'm nowhere near everyone's cup of tea visually. When I say this girl was a bona-fide dime I mean that. Hair was amazing and natural and smelled good, like fruits from a bowl white people make natives carry them on island vacations. She has full lips that are as soft as clouds, but neither as passive nor as wholesome. She was like 5'10" and her legs were long and brown and smooth as I-95 once you're outside of the city limits.

She had her own place and we'd watch Game of Thrones and she'd let me pause and nerd out while she rubbed my back. She'd have been a perfect candidate for a girlfriend, if I didn't already have one I was hiding.

Anyway, we were at Sheffield's, playing pool. There she was, this amazon queen goddess, and here I am a troll with a quick tongue and the devil's luck and it's down to my 8 ball and her striped 14.

If she sinks it, we're tied, and I'm sweating.

I have to beat her. I can't allow her to win, with a girl like this; any error made on my behalf is curtains. Any ineptness is her cue to exit. She wanted an alpha, and alphas can't lose at the pool.

I end up sinking that shot and I let out a shout and I look over and she's hurt she lost and she's salty cause she knows she can't leave yet. I'm still in charge. I'm still calling the fucking shots. Then I pay for the 75 dollar tab and the GrubHub from the Thai place I told her I don't like but she wants it so fuck what I like and now I'm sure she's like yeah you little dumbass have your little game of billiards just foot the bill for the hooch and food.

I thought about this memory as I was playing pool by myself a few weeks ago. I think about this every time I play pool honestly. Partially because she seemed like the ideal partner, but I opted out, to play pool alone.

Idk why I did that.

Just a Wiccan Phase

I can always tell a Wiccan when I see one. I've never been surprised when someone tells me "I practice Wicca." I usually say "Yeah, I get that vibe from you. You're wearing 13 earrings with planets and star pendants. You've got on a black mesh top and a velvet dress and it's the summer. You're pale and have an eyebrow piercing, and you smoke Pall Malls. I gathered you were a Wiccan."

Wiccans look like they work at the kiosk in the mall that sells amethyst and charms and inkwell pens, but on their break they go to the food court and ask Steak and Shake employees for lighters.

Aren't you a witch, how come you can't use fire magick to light your cigarette? Why do you spell magic with a k? Why do you drive your dad's Volvo to work? Where is your broom? You're the lamest fucking warlock I've ever seen.

White people love creating shit to make themselves feel more unique. Since they can't feel division on the basis of skin color, they base their existence on completely insane beliefs so they can hate and judge someone else with an inane belief that contradicts their own. We have to question more shit. You can't come to me and say you're a Wiccan and then not be able to, like, tell me an ancient prophecy. Does the prophecy tell you're going to die a virgin?

Look, I'm a Catholic, I'm not trying to pick on Wicca because Catholicism is stupid too. Yesterday, there was footage of a speech the Pope gave on the news. There was a parade, dudes in armor, and tens of thousands of people. The Pope came out and in typical Catholic fashion, read dryly from an essay he wrote and he essentially just said Palestine and Israel should be cool with each other, African Genocide needs to stop, and we should band together in times of fear. Then he went back into his giant castle and everyone clapped and another parade happened. And that was on the news! A dude who lives in an Italian castle, who we collectively acknowledge as the boss of Christianity just said the most basic shit, dropped the mic, and made it on global news.

My future needs an Allen wrench

A student asked me "Mr. Lawson, can you bring in some magazines? " We're making vision boards in Ms. Phillips class and all she has is furniture magazines." And it was funny to think about how their futures are just pictures of ottomans. The South Side is a sad, underserved and darkly funny place.

Lenny

My hairstylist, after ten years of almost never asking me a personal question, two hours into twisting my hair in silence, asked me on the way out "You went to the Star Wars thing last weekend?" I didn't have a Star Wars shirt on, I never mentioned Star Wars, and he didn't ask me so much as he accused me with a tacit inflection to mimic a question.

No, Lenny, I didn't go to the Star Wars convention.

 What about me says at the Star Wars Convention? Can you smell convention enthusiast in me? Do I smell like Doritos and sweat? I probably do actually. Don't answer that.

You just took a shit in your favorite pizzeria and had to rush out because you didn't want to be link to it (Fecal Racketeering)

You just took a shit. Well I'm getting ahead of myself.

You're off of work and while it wasn't terrible by any stretch, and you know the anatomy of a terrible day, it still sort of sucked. This wasn't a terrible day, it just wasn't a particularly successful one, and when you're in the field you're in (you teach an AP Literature course) not feeling successful in your applications in teaching children can feel spiritually excavating.

On your train ride you sit behind a girl with jet black hair. You once read that black hair is rare in America, and that most times what we see has black is really just a deep brown with a deceptive iridescence, like a raven's wing. You sit behind this woman with this black hair and you think, faintly, of hair dye and the sort of mentality of someone who would actually buy black hair dye (Goths or actors but what's the actual difference between those two subsets of folk.)

She is seated next to a huge man in the linty grey hoodie, they talk about Fruits Baskets, an Anime you've heard of since you've heard of anime but have no interest in watching.

You don't have many interests these days, some days you feel your heart has reached its acceptable mileage limit. Sometimes you think you need to go further and roll over the odometer.

You get off the train before the black hair girl and her giant friend, so their story, and whatever it could have meant to you is cut short, but even as you edit this, a year after writing, you can still see the two. And that's just maybe more a testament to journaling than anything remarkable about those two.

You use the escalator out of the train station even though you should use the stairs. You buy a bag of Cheetos even though you have fruit at your apartment. You light a cigarette even though you signed up for a charity run at your work and you now snore like a character in a Hannah Barbara cartoon. Even though smoking cigarettes upsets the membrane in your throat and nose and causes the snoring. Even though smoking is a leading cause of sleep apnea, a condition your ex-girlfriend had, the only reason that is relevant is because you've spent more time next to her in bed then you have any other human being, and we spend roughly 33% of our lives sleeping, and you feel that's significant for me to mention for you. You walk, slower than usual, you know this because two people march past you and you're in tuned with the subtle irritation of others/delusional cogitations that you can tell they think of you as one of those dreaded, "slow walkers." You're walking slowly because nothing particularly exciting is waiting for you at home, no loving embrace upon entrance, not even a cat to intentionally ignore you exists, only laundry on the floor and dishes to wash and papers to grade.

Some days the odometer seems stagnant.

You stop by Dante's pizza, you almost don't, you almost go home, but you go to Dante's Pizzeria (2825 N Milwaukee Ave, Chicago, IL) and you order too much (A chicken wing basket, a slice of pepperoni, and a beer.) The cashier punches in your order with a back of a felt pen, you hate this, this takes a long time and you hate this, it takes long and he has the use of his fingers, why not just use your fingers, you think? Then you think about how critical you're being. You sit down with your beer, the glass is pleasantly cold, you think you can relax for a little, bade off the pelting reality of responsibility for a little while at least. With Pizza and a beer, on the TV they watch My Hero Academia, an anime you'd said you would watch but you haven't yet, because the world lost some of its color some time ago, and anime, along with your harmonica and exercise, seems like something only happy people can enjoy, and you aren't very happy.

Your mom buys you a harmonica every 2 or 3 Christmases, hoping desperately you'll play them.

You sip the beer and adjust your hat in the mirror a little before the familiar garble of moving bowels alerts you. Alert isn't an onomatopoeia but it should be.

Sometimes the odometer on your heart seems to be at an alarming number, the kind of number the even the most convincing, seasoned, scurrilous car salesmen couldn't turn a profit on, sometimes your spirit feels like this shirt your mom used to use as a pajama shirt, or a shirt she'd wear while cleaning the house on a Sunday afternoon. The shirt was a faded yellow, like the jaundice of the skin, faded like the perimeters around Donald

Trump's eyes. You can tell he wears the tanning goggles. Where is skin cancer when you need it? And had letters on it, but the letters through years of sweat and bleach were peeling off and it left speckled blue remnants of a message that used to be important. Family Reunion 94 or something, but the 4 washed and looked like a pale azure less than Artemtic symbol.

You take such a hard, rancid, shit that sticks to the sides of the bowl. There is no tissue, instead, a stack of table napkins, 1 ply, you've had experience with alternatives methods of butt wiping, in college you'd wipe your ass with socks or printer paper, and you know with 1 ply napkin your fingers ran the very serious risk of puncturing the fabric, jutting up your asshole, and tainting your fingers with recycled waste.

You layer the 1 ply and begin to wipe. It's unglamorous, even as far a wiping goes, you are trepidacious, you are nervous and disgusted and you lose your appetite. And you love Dante's pizza, it's grease and the way the glass of beer always looks like ice cold, amber colored gold. And here you are, defiling this place with a shit that seems more like the shit of a Confederate soldier on a drunken night at a latrine then it does the shit of a modern man in a modern world of handheld supercomputers.

You think about the girl on the train, you think about liquid gold, you think about all the boys and girls who grocery shop for one. You think about how all it would take to make someone's day is a hug or a conversation over coffee. You think about how people remember your name, and sometimes are glad to see you, even in passing.

You feel the needle on the odometer spike a little.

Swearengen

You had initially left me on read. Which is common for me, pretty girls are inundated with propositions from men far more attractive and far more capable of fantastical financial feats than I am, I get it.

It seems like every pretty girl in Chicago knows a guy with a boat, and when summer hits then Instagram is full of videos of girls with ear to ear smiles and tongues stuck out like slutty iguanas, twerking on the starboard of some finance execs boat. And I watch and send heart emojis from under the fan in my bedroom.

Then a few months later I ran into you at The Promontory and you smiled at me. You have my all-time favorite smile. The key to a good smile is the shimmer in the eye that denotes actual joy. When you smile you almost look like you've been caught by surprise by how happy you are. I wish I would have known how much I'd miss you smile, I'd of spent more time trying to crack you up, I'm quite good at it.

Some months later you'd tell me that you never once paid for her own tab when you were at The Promontory. That you always ended up finding a man to foot the bill for her food and drinks. Which is an impressive feat, The Promontory is expensive and you drink a lot. I found that out that night because I was the guy who bought your drinks. I don't remember what we talked about but I do remember the way you talk: in those long sentences, no detail missed or omitted. I found myself lost in your details, like reading a good book. In that moment I knew I had to make something of us, God ain't in the habit of giving me that much ease in my trembling spirit without having a purpose for it.

I didn't realize I was falling in love with you until the night we turned off the TV and read our books on the couch. After about 45 minutes I looked over and noticed you were softly sleeping.

A month later and we are intimate with our bodies and a month after that I finally get you to talk in that candid way that lovers do. That deep sorta talking you do with your head on a pillow and you're so close the other person might as well be wearing a sweater stitched with your skin. You might as well be in a pool consisting of the liquefied qualities of their essence. Swimming the canal of them, bathed in them, dripping with them.

 You had dreams of moving to Los Angeles where you'd be a muse to a rock star or something. You were always going on about the 'big fish', a man with wealth and incredible means to find you, keep you, fuck you and feed you and then when it was all said done you told me that we'd reconnect and you'd let me live with you on the farm you got from the divorce settlement. In my own room though, you made that clear. I wasn't the 'big fish' for you and that hurt my ego, but I ain't ever going to fault you for your honesty. I believe you were always honest with me. You made it clear that you'd never be mine to possess.

Being with you was like trying to lasso a hurricane, while blindfolded and facing the wrong direction with no working knowledge on how lassos work or even how to tie the appropriate knots. Trying to have you was akin to the impossibility of trying lasso wind.

I didn't like the way you treated me sometimes. Like I was an afterthought. I was always something you'd squeeze into your schedule before or after something. I felt like a dentist appointment and not your partner.

You felt aloof most of the time, sometimes it even felt as if it was accidental, like you'd hadn't considered me at all. I found that confounding and intoxicating. But admittedly I get very quick, when I'm in that is. I treat women like teenagers treat bands, I hear a song I like by the artist then I listen to the whole catalog. I study every note and key change and lyric. I learn the member's names, I watch interviews and different live performances of the same song to see if I notice different flourishes during certain lines. When I meet a girl I like it's akin to when the weird kid in high school discovered Slipknot, all of a sudden its black nails, mesh and everyone is heartless and stupid besides them and Slipknot. It's flattering when but it doesn't necessarily read as 'healthy' when it's attributed to a woman who is (often) (nearly) a stranger.

I'd broken things off with you at a party while I was wasted. It had been on my mind to do so for a while. This was my first time initiating a formal break up, usually I'm the one dissatisfactory party who gets the boot. This was my first inkling that we were doomed. Although I woke up the next morning, regretting my decision. Surely you'd come around and be my girl like I wanted you too eventually. I called you frantically.

Sometimes when I get to thinking about people and situations and how lives divulge and how many exes I can't reach out to and it's like I've lost a part of myself. Like a version of me is still with them and I can't access it, like I was once a full pizza, and now I'm just the skinny slices and the gnawed on ends.

When you picked up you told me you had to walk around the block a few times, then you told me you didn't want to see me romantically anymore. Then you told me that I was favorite and you thought we were learning to love each other and having fun along the way.

This reminded me of a time in an Uber when you looked at me and told me you were falling for me. And I don't think you ever lied to me. The truth is I was great to you because you were my penance to the universe for all the hell I'd put women through. I tried so hard with you, every step of the way and I don't regret it, but it did hurt that even with my best concerted effort I was still a candidate to be abandoned.

 Two weeks later you asked to come over and I thought it was to finally pick up your earmuffs and Frank Ocean record. You called me and told me you wanted to see me, and you almost never said that, that you wanted to see me. I always felt like meeting up with you was like fishing for Apache Trout. Not that I know fuck all about fishing but I heard that the Apache Trout are in the top 4 rarest American fishes. I know a bunch of random facts. Anyway getting you to want to spend time with me usually required food or drugs, often both, and in those rare moments when I'd wake up next to you, I'd feel like I'd won something. Won the attention, albeit temporary, of someone truly special.

When you came over you disrobed and sat next to me on the couch and told me you were pregnant. You spent the next two weeks with me.

Your skin would be so hot, like a radiator wrapped in flesh. You were running a temperature, I'd feel it emitting off of you in bed late at night and I'd take the blanket off you. Most days you couldn't get out of bed because you felt like shit, you were sluggish, and your eyes had a narcotized drowsy quality to them like you'd taken too much cough medicine. You'd breathe out of your mouth and when I looked at you it was like I was looking at a husk of you. You'd spend the first 5 hours of every day grimacing or puking or looking like there was the spiritual equivalent of popcorn stuck in your teeth. You'd lost your job because you felt so shitty.

You were a dog walker on the North Side. A cold, unrelenting job that saw you traveling from affluent brownstone to marble countered condo, walking the dogs of people who could afford such extravagances. You also had a roommate who's main source of income was a 4 month old lump sum payment from his father's will, that he only received a fraction of due to burial expenses and other litigations.

I think seeing those homes, with their fleets of rumbas and their sliding glass shower doors, inspired you in a lot of ways. Showed you glimpses of what life could be, like a ghost haunting a mansion, all the while taking an inventory of all you wanted when God chose you for reincarnation. Assuming he wouldn't choose to reincarnate you as an animal. Imagine making a list of nifty appliances to strive for upon the opportunity then you get placed in the body of a mongoose.

I'd run to Target 3 times a day when you stayed at my apartment that week, restocking on apple slices, pomegranate juice, Dramamine etc. One time you called me as I was already leaving the Target to buy corn dogs because you had a craving. You sounded so pitiful on the phone, it was so different from the confident timbre I usually heard, and was intimidated by, in your voice. So I got you corndogs and made them and you ate them in my bed in your underwear and I moved to caress your butt and you turned around and looked at me and said:

"If you don't stop sexualizing me I'm going to kill you.' And just like that, the pitiful quality was gone.

And you never used threatening language, I think because of your Dad, who you'd told me so many things about. How sometimes you felt scared around him. How when you were a kid and you messed up he'd make you squat while holding dictionaries. How before he hit you with belts you'd run and when he caught you, he'd drag you back.

One time we were fighting on my living room floor and you told me you were getting triggered so we had to stop. I lay on the floor and you got on top of me and I tried to back bridge with you on top of me and I got really close before my weak arms gave out. You looked down at me with the same smile from 4 months ago, and it felt like every had been just a day ago. You made me remember every detail, with your smiles and your long sentences.

You came over and we on my couch and we were okay, you told me you swore off sex, I was afraid you were going to swear off me. I couldn't let you do that.

We cried in bed for around two hours. You told me about how you could feel them, keenly in your body, how your senses were heightened, you were becoming a super human in front me. You were housing twins, my twins.

'I don't know if I want to get rid of them.'

'Maybe we don't have to.' I said. Then you looked up at me, I could feel the air from your nostrils blowing on the wet spot that your tears left on my stomach. You looked up at me and this portal opened up somewhere in your mind. You were running with the idea of having our twins and living a life with me and I finally thought I'd lasso'd the hurricane.

Then you turned away, I could no longer feel your cold breaths, we stayed silent for a while. We were so good at taking our time weren't we? You stared off for a while and I stared at you, hoping against hell you'd look up at me and you'd agree to keep them. So we could be together, and I know that would get in the way of your Los Angeles trip, and I know I'm not the biggest fish yet and I know you're 23 and so far out of my league its considered community service when you fuck me. I know its stupid for me to think I could afford twins, I know its stupid to have kids with barely know and isn't committed to you, but everyone seems to do stupid shit all the time that pans out for them.

Its high time some stupid shit worked out for me too.

'I can't right now.' You said almost like an apology.

"I know, and that's ok." I whimper, accepting your apology. 'You can feel them?'

'Yeah..' you said on a weakened outbreath.

'What does it feel like.'

'It's nearly impossible to describe. I just know I'll never be alone again.'

Another silence settles into the room as we both cry.

"Where will they go?"

"I think they will wait for us in different lives. I think they know we aren't ready and I think their souls will find us later."

You spoke with this certainty, like you were in communion with somewhere far grander than this liminal fourth dimension. You spoke with ancient wisdom.

"They won't be mad if we make them wait."

"They've already forgiven us." You say and I start sobbing. And it's hard talking about it now because sometimes I close my eyes to sleep and I see two small silhouettes and it's just like you said, they're waiting for me to be ready. Part of me feels incomplete, and I'm sure it's more powerful to you. They were part of your personhood. A part you wanted but couldn't have I think. Hats another thing that breaks my heart, I think you wanted

That weekend, they were gone. And I knew in most ways our story was over.

And that's bummer, because I put away my lasso, and I know you aren't a hurricane. Just a girl with shit to do, and I was lucky to be part of that shit.

Call me.

Part 2

Full on loss of composure

One time a girl told me she had taken ecstasy 3 nights in a row and instead of address the obvious health risks that go with such habitual drug use can cause, I thought about how even after 3 waves of elevated serotonin I didn't get a frantic, misspelled text message professing love, or at the very least a photo of a titty.

Was I not worthy of a few characters, a few mere strokes across the keyboard? I'm a simple man, like Lynyrd Skynyrd told me to be.

Jungle Rot 1

I bet the majority of people have seen one of if not both of their parents naked at one point. Outside of the more serious, purposeful situations, like having to bathe a sick parent on hospice, I bet a lot of the instances of parental nudity are out of convenience, while at an early age.

In the case of my own father he literally never used a drying towel, and after showering, he'd walk past me, stark naked, as I lay on his bed to watch the only TV in our home that had cable. My father's chode was the price I had to pay to watch Ren and Stimpy.

To this day I still remember my father flamingo walking past the television naked.

People walk differently when they're naked. Either in a shy way, with more restrained, cautious movements, as if those smaller movements caused invisibility, or they walk around in airy, free way. A way that resembles a snowflake's descent from heaven, riding the wind with an insouciant ease.

I'm not sure what my father's flamingo walk said about him, but I do know the act felt like the silent displays of love that Midwestern boys grow up with. Who needs words or affirmation or a ball to throw around in the backyard when you have a full view of a chode?

As I child I had strange understanding of sex, informed in large parts by the secrecy and censoring my parents would employ when an inevitable sex scene appeared in film during family movie night. My mom would cover my eyes, but never my ears, so I could hear the music, slow and orchestral with these mighty triumphant crescendos. If it was a particularly spicy scene, I could hear sharp exhalations, like Tinkerbell trying to catch their breath. When the scene was over, her hands would free my vision and the characters would be laying down and peering into each other's drowsy eyes with grins.

I knew, instinctually and primordially, that whatever act had occurred beyond my vision had something to do with chodes, like my fathers. I knew that when I grew up and I had a chode of my very own that I'd lay down with someone and harps would play and Tinkerbell would gasp.

In many ways that was the pinnacle of my closeness with my father; the strongest our bond has ever been was in those moments of vulnerability and trust. No words were needed.

As time progressed, I got older and I realized harps don't play when you fuck, not every time atleast.

Instead of harps, most of the time it's an episode of Black Mirror as the background soundtrack because I can't make it through an hour of that depressing meandering show without needing some consensual fornicating to uplift me.

As time progressed and as most sons do, I came into the awareness that my dad was a flawed man in a great many ways and this forced me to take on mental shifts. We went from two war buddies in barracks to, at best, contentious roommates. At worst, near strangers.

When I was in High School, our dichotomy was truly volatile, and our house was the arena to a great many domestic battles.

My father is self-proclaimed "smart-dumb mother fucker" and I'm inclined to agree with that assertion.   He says he never did remarkably great in school. Partially due to his dyslexia, which I'm under the impression had no real treatment available, at least not to black boys living during the tail end of Jim Crow. His vision was so poor that when he enlisted in the service, he was denied his original request to be a war time photographer and instead was dispatched to Vietnam as Air Force Infantry.

In America, poor vision discards you from shooting a Nikon but not an M-14 rifle, I guess.

Once during family movie night, I proposed watching Pan's Labyrinth.

"Doesn't that movie have subtitles?" My father questioned.

"What, you can't read?" I snapped back at him, so ensconced in my own misplaced anger that his desyia did not register. Even though I had heard the story of his postponed photography career and subsequent life as a soldier many times.

I don't think I'll ever forget the way he looked up at me with his glazed over face. The only thing preventing him from leaping up and choking me was the knowledge that it wouldn't change anything.

These miniature civil wars broke out through the duration of high school and when it was time to pack up for college, I closed the door emotionally on a lot of things. My dad was one of them. We've spent the last 5 or 6 years fairly distant.

One of two things happens when you ice out a parent :Either you dump that built up reservoir of love on others; partners or students or pets, dousing them with it, sometimes to your own detriment.

Or you withdraw, keep everyone at arms distance like a boxer. Allowing no one to orbit too close for fear of collision. All that love you don't share sticks to your sides and clogs you up. Like spiritual soap scum.

I oscillate between both of these, sharing with the wrong people and keeping everyone in the dark. Depending on the day or how much I'd had to drink, I was either over sharing or making commitments in my head to get buried with the inner machinations of my heart.

That was until mine was a case of jungle rot.

Jungle Rot 2

I had been hobbling around the hallways of my work and along the streets of my neighborhood for around a week until I was diagnosed with Jungle Rot. The first few days of the limp, I had actually thought it a character adding condition. I felt like Dr. Gregory House, despondently cool and world-weary. I even mulled over the idea of getting a cane.

I thought it was a sex related injury, I thought I had pulled a muscle from putting in that good stroke work.I thought I'd fornicated myself into pain, as I am one to do. The primary difference with this instance of coitus borne pain is that unlike the normal coitus born pain I feel, this one was physical.

 I had even arrogantly attributed the limp to my modest leg workout with the wrestling team. I'm a literature teacher at a high school and nothing says I'm a literature teacher like getting a limp from three minutes of squats.

On my fifth day with the limp, I noticed specks of blood spotting my underwear. I reacted with the extreme fear that leads frantic questioning.

 What on my body, in such a high priority area, is bleeding? Is this apoplexy? Have I finally become a woman?

 After finishing the day, admittedly less than involved with my students' work, I called my parents.

We were reading A Streetcar Named Desire and I'd never known turmoil quite like listening to three hours of terrible Louisiana accents while something in my nether region bled.

"Hi Bootsy I was wondering when you were going to call your poor old mother." My mom calls me Bootsy, and we can get into where that came from at a later date.

"Hi mom, how is everything?"

"Everything is fine Bootsy, how are you?"

"Well, I think my penis is bleeding."

"What?" My mother's mock, sing-song, parody version of a voice gives way to one of shock and horror.

I explain that I found specks of blood in my underwear and I say that I'm in an Uber to their house.

But this decision doesn't come easy. I had a date with Ina that evening.

Ina was an empirically pretty girl. Her skin looked grey in some photos. Even in her peaked tone she still had warm, round cheeks and a smile where she squinted her eyes so hard it seemed like she was trying to sequester an inferno exploding behind her eyelids. I really liked her smile.

She was also stacked like a Denny's Grand Slam. She was from Baton Rouge and wore overalls and mom pants most the time, priding herself in modest, practical wear. Real archaic Bible belt shit, but once I saw her in leggings that clung to her ass like Alex Honnold clung to El Captain's peak at Yosemite. I wanted very much to peel those leggings down and dive into her like kids dive for candy after the piñata busts.

One of my first memories is being at a birthday party with a piñata, watching it break and the subsequent frenzy of children crashing into one another to round up as many tootsie rolls as they could. I didn't dive, so my mom gave me a push and I scanned the perimeter for stray candy. I like to apply this strategy to my adult life. The epicenters of things are nothing more than messy melees, it's on the outskirts that I've found what I need.

When I would see Ina out, at community events or gallery openings or outside one of the many bars on Milwaukee Ave in the blessed year of our Lord, 2016, I'd catch myself staring, and not always for the scandalous reasons above. Sometimes I'd catch myself staring the way you stare at a painting, noticing something smaller and more impressive each time. Ina would often catch me staring, opting to slyly smirk or to ignore me all together.

I went to her birthday party one fall night and she was nice and drunk. She whispered in my ear "I want you to tell me everything that makes you sad." Then spun me around and sang "Temperature" by Sean Paul as she played bongos on my butt. It was at that moments that I realized that women are strong candidates to be fuck boys as well.

After the booty bongos, I got brave and I asked her out to a movie. She accepted. She canceled her fitness class, and if it was anything other than a 7 PM fitness class I would have been flattered. We saw a Yorgos Lanthimos film and if you've seen any Yorgos Lanthimos films, then you know they are characterized by eerie ambient soundtracks and starling displays of violence. At no point did I feel compelled to make a move, even the act of eating popcorn seemed out of place.

It wasn't until two weeks until I asked her out again. I work slowly, due in some part to my belief that love at sixteen passive glance is infinitely more romantic than love at first sight. Love at first sight seems nice on paper. Like being caught in a net. A dreamy nylon mesh of feelings contorting and ensnaring your heart. But I think what's most appealing about love at first sight to people is how easy it seems. You've let go of the wheel and chemicals and endorphins take over, the maintenance and vulnerability and intention and luck it takes to actually fall in love fades away. Love at first sight is like a free buffet with a thick ankled country gal beating a skillet with a ladle shouting, "Come and get it."

In my experience, love is almost never a buffet. It's a diner where a lot of the items on the menu aren't available or they are seasonal, so you have to wait a few months. Love for me is a restaurant with inconvenient hours and fickle wait staff. It's a drive through at 3 AM and you order too much and the leftovers don't keep so they spoil in the fridge but you don't throw them out right away because you have good memories attached to them and they make your otherwise empty fridge seem like it has food. They make it seem full. I prefer spoiled quesadillas to cold, white emptiness.

I've been really good with food metaphors since the 90s.

Through some charismatic subterfuge on my part, or morbid curiosity on hers, Ina agrees to dinner with me. A much more intimate parameter, one where I could gaze at the smile when my jokes landed and one where she could, I don't know, extract whatever abstract joy women get from looking at me. My mustache grows uneven and It's a form of assault having anyone look at me when I'm eating something I enjoy eating. The grisly, primitive way I assault chicken wings matches the Cookie Monster's annihilation of cookies or Goku's oral molestation of ramen and rice.

My first thought, after the obligatory "Dear God my dick is bleeding, something is acutely, wrong, I'm done for, my penis and balls are spattered in blood, is this a Cannibal Corpse song. Am I living a Cannibal Corpse song?" was:

"What about Ina? Ina and I have a date lined up. Ina could have been the one," I thought.

Dear woman I've given the code name of Ina to, if you possess the keen eye to see yourself in this story, and maybe you will : it's a credit to your beauty that even as y penis bled, I still thought about limping my way to you. So even though things never panned out, you can at least have that.

Ina would have to wait, I needed now to get to the bottom of this crimson colored genitial discharge. I get a Lyft to my parents house, my mother is a career nurse but when I got to house she deferred all penis bleeding remedies to my Dad who, and this is going to be the first nice thing I say about my father in my writing, potentially ever, and I'll be sure to talk to my social worker about that, one of those dying breed of men who can do everything, which is particularly impressive because he grew up without the infinite knowledge the internet bestows on us, that this generation of men narry takes advantage of.

He is a relic, holding the gritty knowledge of distant jungles in his hands, those same hands would later be holding a flashlight to my balls and spot a laceration between my ball sack and leg.

Upon arriving at my parents house, my mom hugs me and says that she'll be the backup, that if my father really needed her expertise, then she'd volunteer it. I'm sure the sight of her son's testicles weren't exactly a sight she longed to see. not on some idle Tuesday in the spring.

It was a Tuesday, which leads me to believe that it was never in fact a date with Ida, no one wants their hearts opened to the grand possibility of love on Tuesdays, most Tuesdays I want to be put into a walking comatose until Friday.

  My dad tells me to go up stairs and to take off my pants. A request I hope I never hear from a 69 year old man again.

As I lay in the bed I'd lay in as a child, my pants off, and a towel covering my dick, which seemed like the most appropriate thing to do, I remember watching my dad flamingo walking past me in the nude as a child.

I thought about how I remembered those moments, clear and crips as if watching a film playback of them. I remembered laying in this very position, on my moms side of the bed. The same smell of Karl Laherfield and scented perfumes that saturate my parents room, pungent to my nostrils, like they were when I was a kid, and all those dark years of teenage angst and early twenties ire melt away, into something old and ancient, like my dad, like the love between a father and a son.

My dad comes into the room, with a plastic bag of medic equipment and the previously mentioned industrial flashlight that he uses to illuminate the jungle of hair and taint that is his son's nethers.

It's also important to note that the washcloth I use to cover my dick is a means of embarrassment based on modesty at the size of my non-erect peter, I wouldn't want my dad thinking he raised a weak dicked son. I assure you he has not.

When he came into the room I felt a bizarre melding of energy. I lay on the bed with some macabre eagerness, partially because I knew I was in the hands of the only two people I can trust in the world, and partially because I was writing this book and knew my father doing amatue I could feel a sense of elation reverberating off of him. Something happens to the eyes when a person understands that duty calls. I saw the same look of regrettable responsibility in my parents eyes when they talked about funeral arrangements for my grandmother. It's a distant look, almost like you're watching a fatal car wreck and knowing that

When my dad was in his 50s he, like all men in their 50s if not younger should, got a colonoscopy. Part of the procedure, if you opt for it, is anesthetic so severe that patients tend to be in a loopy state for several hours. I was in college and didn't have a driver's license so my Dad asked my cousin to be the designated driver after the operation. I resented that I couldn't fulfill that for my dad, I thought it would be good bonding, my dad rattling off things in a heavily narcotized state and me coming to realization and conclusions, but I couldn't share that, so I lay in bed thinking this would be an alternative bonding expense.

Now I'm sure some of you are reading this like why now go golfing why does bonding with you have to relate to narcotics and genitals, and If I'm being candid, that's my comfort zone, I'll also bring that up with my social worker, I don't know what's going on with me most days.

After mere seconds of observing my testicles under the harsh unforgiving flashlight he had assessed the injury as something he'd seen in Vietnam called Jungle Rot, also known clinically as a Tropical Ulcer. Now he was slightly off, what he saw was a deep lesion in the crevice between my leg and my ball sack, caused by wearing tight pants and having coarse pubic hair. Throughout the day the tightness of my pants constricted my walk causing the hair to rub and open up a lesion. Full on jungle rot is when micro bacteria infects the wound. My dad told me anecdotes as he observed the cut about how other GIs would need to get amputated for jungle rot.

I always loved my Dad's jungle stories;

When I was a kid he'd tell me this story about a monkey he and the rest of the men kept, he said that feed it crackers then one day they put it in a cage so it would escape and they could play with it and observe it everyday. He told me one day they woke up and a snake had eaten the monkey, but the monkey had not yet disgusted the snake's belly so it was stuck in the cage, unable to squeeze through the bars. He said the men wasted no time in killing the snake. He said they all nevr understood why they caged the snake in the first place, they fed it everyday when it was free. It would have come back regardless of the cage.

Avoid caging things, for fear of snakes.

My dad told me to apply ointment to the cut and wear looser pants. I spent the night with my parents. I told Ina I couldn't make it that evening, that it was a funny story and that I'd tell her one day. She left me on read and we really don't talk now.

This is me telling her, and you.

Cornbread

Once when I was in high school a man from the next block (I call him a man because he was at least twenty-four) named Cornbread rang my doorbell asking for me. My parents, confused, called me to the door, where Cornbread motioned for me to walk with him. He then began a lengthy, convoluted, cryptic, diatribe about how he wasn't a "nigga to be played with," and how he's not afraid to "tell my parents." Cornbread was one of the many sketchy neighborhood dudes I got involved with when I was fifteen in my pursuit of Nastasha.

Natasha was new to the block and lived with her aunt in the house on the corner and had this pristine, brown skin and she was my virginal, pubescent obsession. I'd walk to the corner store with her, she'd ring my doorbell to play with my dog (never me, and I believed her. I really think she liked my dog way more than me, I don't think it was an excuse to see me. I think she loved Streak and I was just a sweaty, pervy, attendant to my dog.) I was positively in love with Natasha and in my (futile, foolish) pursuit of her I met a lot of dudes who were fucking weird.

And now one, perhaps the weirdest, Cornbread, who again was at least twenty-four but hung out with us high schoolers, was at my doorstep acting erratic and alarming. He was claiming I'd stiffed him on a bag of weed, and now he was livid and like any narcotics dealer worth his salt, was looking for recompense. Only thing is, this drug dealer wasn't threatening to break my legs, he was threatening to tell my parents. Also, I'd never bought weed from Cornbread, or at least I now, at twenty-seven can't remember ever taking weed from Cornbread with assurances of payment at a later date. Also, maybe don't front teenagers. Also, maybe don't sell to teenagers? Also, this was 2005 on the south side of Chicago, everything was reggie, ditch weed, schwag. That's all we knew and you could get three blunts worth $20.

You gonna tell my parents for $20? That's crazy. I remember nodding a lot. Thinking about Nastasha, and how of course a girl as fine as she was would know the neighborhood roughnecks well and certainly develop feelings for them. How could I compete with them? They sold weed. I got an allowance for trash and good grades, and I never got good grades, so I never had much money. And I wasn't tough, I'm letting Cornbread punk me, and his name is Cornbread.

Eventually our conversation ended, and Cornbread walked back to his house. For two years every time I heard the doorbell ring, I'd think 'Oh Fuck its Cornbread. He's gonna tell my parents.'

It never was Cornbread, and now his old house is boarded up, Nastasha stopped coming over asking to walk my dog, I guess having me as a collateral creep got too much, the cons outweigh the pros.

I never heard much about Cornbread or Natasha, people have a way of disappearing in my neighborhood. They disappear there and they disappear away.

4 inches from love.

The best part about Estelle's American Boy is that she says she found a 5'7 guy who's just her type. She showed love to shorter boys.

As a 5'7 guy let me tell you it's rough out here. There's a lot of stuff we can't reach and no one really notices you when you walk into a room. Do you know how loud and how flamboyant my shirts have to be to get noticed? I gotta dress like I'm in the fucking Migos to draw the eye. Like a peacock, a small, resentful peacock who just wants a seat at the table.

Plus, I'm going to be old and the same height. No one's grandpa is 5'7, Imma look like Papa Smurf or Gimli from Lord of The Rings. What if my son is like 18 one day and there's that pivotal father-son moment where there's a heated argument and he's like entering manhood, you know, and he challenges me and heavens forbid it comes to blows but if it does the father has to beat the son up. What if my son is taller than me, some long necked, lanky freak who's like 6'2? I'd have to use a weapon. Then all my son's life he'd tell people that his father threw ninja blinding powder in his eyes and choked him on the floor with a tie. 5'7 is a transient height, it's like a fifteen-year-old's height before he tops out at like 5'11.

No one should stop at 5'7. You either finish growing at 5'5 and resign to being short but you get a great job and work out, or you're blessed and you grow to like 6'2 and life is just made easy for you like "Hey I'm 6'2 and I'm here for infinite female attention and respect for the rest of my life." Also why do all 6'2 people smell the same? Like this flat smelling sock smell, like not bad, but like very similar. Like light sweat and un-originality.

The most impressive move I've seen pulled off in the club was by a good friend of mine at Reggae Night at Sub-T. If you've been to Reggae Night then you know that it can get filled up with some pretty tough customers, and when my crew would go we don't really read "tough" we sort of read "Latte with almond milk." We don't read "street," we are serving "LAN party and Mountain Dew" vibes.

I don't give a shit about reggae, I almost hate reggae. But I'm not there for the music I'm there for the women and the dutty winin', ya know.

Anyway, this couple walks past us, the man is leading the charge, holding the girl's hand, and he probably thinks he's doing a great job. Asserting himself, taking the lead, probably really proud or whatever. Then my friend grabs her other hand, slyly, without her boo noticing, but not like he cares about the boo, he grabs her hand as if to say; "this ain't about him." And she smiles so hard it almost cracks her face in two. He wasn't even trying to pull her, it was just a physical hello. And my friend is skinny and 6'3 and from what little I've been able to ascertain about women, that's pretty much all you need to be. (Which makes shit really hard for me, you know, I'm 5'7, do you know how much extra shit I have to do? Buy cowboy shirts and shit.) And no matter how that girls night ended, no matter if she got married to that guy, every argument they have, every doubt that enters her mind is going to be book ended by thoughts of my friend and how secret and taboo and bad/great it made her feel. It was magical.

Champagnepapi for my real friends.

I knew Aubrey Graham as Jimmy from the 2nd iteration of Canada's seminal teenage propagandist prime-time melodrama, Degrassi High: The Next Generation. (One could argue this was a watered down version the United Kingdom's teen drama 'Skins', which is an attempt to serialize and thus financially capitalize on Harmony Karroine's success with the movie 'Kids', which is, yet again, a bastardized and insultingly romanticized version of the actual events of a great many high school age children in urban neighborhoods.) Following in this vein of the glorification of adolescent turmoil, Degrassi tackled a great many issues among the more comical: visible thongs, getting high before a college fair, and abusing laxatives to make weight for the wrestling team.

There were also episodes about the dangers of taking too much meth, as if a little meth is understandable, and finding a dead body.

Showing remarkable duality, Degrassi High also tackled material that felt more pertinent; pro-life debates, the complex nature of sexuality, suicidal ideation, spousal abuse, mental disability, and dating a LARPer.

Aubrey Graham, who currently plays Judeo-Caribbean, Texan, mobster, rapper who moonlights as an R&B artist "Drake", originally played Jimmy on Degrassi. Jimmy was the character with the sexist opinion. ("Just dump that slut.")

Jimmy was the blackest kid in Degrassi high, which really speaks to the diversity at Degrassi High, because Jimmy was half white. He was awarded some level of default-based deference. He became the aficionado of hip hop; he was a gatekeeper of sorts, if black culture was an alternate dimension then Jimmy was the Stargate. Liquid-y and pulsating and sort of gross.

Not so much the best option as it was really the only option.

After Degrassi ended, or more succinctly after I had outgrown it, I didn't hear much from Aubrey Graham. Until he donned the mantle of 'Drake.'

I first began listening to Drake with his song 'Best I ever had' which should be regarded, without dispute as a seminal song of millennial growth. He would go on to release a colossal wave of certified bangers. He rose to prominence at a time where 'Scene' music was being strangled out by autotune and Hip Hop's fashion was transitioning between the baggy and unapproachable, to the skin tight and pacifying. Lil Wayne had begun skateboarding and The Shins were making music for Hollywood movies. Mainstream became counterculture and the counterculture wanted to buy mansions so they sold out. It was a changing of the guard, and Drake was there to usher us in. He represented the spirit of the emo scene but the edge of rap. He was like getting a ride to the mall by your conservative parents but keeping an extra set of 'thug' pants in your book bag to change into.

He was tough, but not really.

Drake came to power in the last few dark months after 'Yeezus' dropped, signifying the end of Kanye being the number one guy in hip hop. Kanye's reign began after Lil Wayne had relinquished the title during his stint on Rikers Island. Wayne had captured the throne after Eminem started getting sober and rapping as Triumphant the Insult Comedy Dog.

We were looking for a new champion, and it didn't matter that he was a Canadian Child Actor.

It wasn't until 'Hotline Bling' dropped that Drake became a cultural phenomenon. He had consumed the world, like Pacman eating whatever the fuck those dots are supposed to represent. Tree trunks of the Amazon stuck in the crevices of his grill, all seven great, salty seas moisturizing his lips.

His iconic status was not dissimilar to hypnosis, but benign Canadian hypnosis. Less cloak and dagger more willful compliance. We let Drake dance and croon and climb neon steps. And before we knew it, he was an insurmountable force. A household name. My dad, a Vietnam vet who confuses all forms of media, once he confused Prince's musical Purple Rain with the film adaptation of Alice Walker's The Color Purple, was able to identify Drake in a Sprite commercial. Maybe Drake was the catalyst to Sprite taking the throne as the most preferred soft drink by African Americans.

 (When I was writing this I ran it by a friend who said Orlando Jones sold Sprite way before Drake and I said that Orlando Jones sold 7 up! And asked him, was he trying to say all clear pops look the same?)

Sometime later, a show hit the internet that became a similar social phenomena and pertinent force in the zeitgeist. That show was Stranger Things, helmed by the stoic and brooding once-in-a-life-time performance of Eleven, portrayed by Millie Bobby Brown.

Through some spider web of Hollywood Hob-Knobbing Millie and Drake become friends, which wouldn't have been cause for alarm, had I not seen an interview with Millie. In which she detailed the workings of their relationship which includes romance advice, dinners, and lamentation of how much they miss one another.

A thirty-one-year-old texting a fourteen-year-old about boy issues is like Dracula texting a mosquito for tips on blood sucking.

The only real advice Drake should be giving Millie about boys her age is what malls have the most lax policy on seeing rated R movies without adult supervision. The only reason a fourteen-year-old should text a thirty-one-year-old is for a letter of recommendation to an AP class. (And being a teacher, I don't even allow my kids to do that, use my email or wait until class, my phone ain't for you child.)

Alarmingly, she admitted in an interview with E! the two had dinner, and here I was ignorant to the fact that Nobu had a kid's menu

Perhaps I'm overreacting, perhaps it is no different than a working relationship; one huge star giving a rising star tutelage. Maybe Drake plays mentor. But, if that's the case, then why have we not heard of other young talents Drake is mentoring? Does he only like "Stranger Things" for Eleven? What about Dustin or Mike or Will? Fuck, I mean, with all due respect, Wynonna Ryder looks like she could use a dinner with Drake? Why this fourteen-year-old girl? Why not an up and coming rapper? Why not me?

Like I said perhaps I'm overreacting. But stars have a long storied history of this predatory behavior; Bowie, Seinfeld, Allen, Elvis, even a hero of mine, JD Salinger, had recorded dalliances with underage girls.

Then there is the Billie Ellish story.

I don't who or where this weird, pale, goth Avril Lavine on Xanax, thing they call Billie Elish came from, or why anyone would listen to any music she makes outside of 'Ocean Eyes', which is a very solid song, but she claims her and Drake also have a texting relationship. Claiming they'd never met, but he texted her out of the blue and the rest is history. Billie Elish is seventeen.

Then there was the Bella Harris date, who at eighteen went on a date with Drake. Bella claims she met Drake for the first time at sixteen.

What the fuck is Drake doing? We root for him, we support him, and we have for so long. He's accessible, he's vulnerable yet braggadocious, he's tough yet sweet, he makes songs for people who want to get drunk and dance as well as for guys who carry guns. He's the personification of crossover appeal. Earlier in the year, we let him get away with having a secret child and having multiple ghost writers. I suppose that's why Drake uses the symbol of the Owl. Owls live within the darkness, symbolizing magic, mystery, and ancient knowledge.

(Drake has a song where he repeats the phrase 'free smoke' 28 times. I felt this was appropriate after attributing him with ancient knowledge.)

Drake is the world's biggest hip hop artist. We allowed this. We let Drake get away with being a child star from Canada and taking the helm of one of the most lucrative, violent, and powerful mediums since the coliseum.

(When are white people going to bring the coliseum back? You guys are so good and breathing life into other antiquated forms of entertainment. Record Players, VHS players, crocheting. When are you all ready to big back something useful like white flight, or the coliseum?)

And yet, he has this discernable pattern of grooming.

When something like this happens we need to launch a volley of questions. In these situations the best cannot be assumed. With wealth, everything in life gets exponentially easier, and that includes our more nefarious proclivities, like preying on children. The rich and elite have a history of it.

Grooming is what they call it, the way kings groom princes, giving them choices, putting them in scenarios they haven't properly matured to handle. The way Zazu groomed Simba and Nala, the way my father groomed me to handle the waves of adulthood that crash upon my shores with frigid frequency. But at the end of this there is no castle to inherit, no family sword or banner to take up. Because the person doing it isn't a king, he's a man who's leading with his dick in interactions with a child. A man abusing trust on a grand, criminal scale.

So next time Drake plays, and he invariably will, consider the bizarre looking Canadian man behind the shuffles and vulnerability.

Like we should have been doing all along.

Solution Oriented.

Or

Stephon Clark was shot 8 times, 6 in the back, implying that he was attempting to run, now normally if someone tries to run, like a child or a dog, you pursue them, also running, in an attempt to stop capture them. I've never been babysitting a child, someone I am tasked to serve and protect, seen them run, and thought 'I'd better shoot this child. How else am I going to stop him?'

Stephon Clark, the 22 year old black man who was shot and killed in 2018 by police while unarmed and in his grandmother's yard, inspired me to think of the perfect solution to quell police suspicion and to ensure the safety of countless black people across America. Since the police have difficulties determining if an object in the hand of a black man is a firearm, then we need to fill our hands with objects that are both easily discernible and pacifying to white people: Basketballs. If every black man carries a basketball around with him at all times, there will be literally no way an officer could assume that black man was armed. You see, Stephon Clark had a white iPhone in his hands when he was murdered. The police officers saw this object, in all its rectangular whiteness. How could they not, with all of their extensive training, that the state (taxpayers) funds, tell if a white iPhone isn't really a glock, or a chainsaw, or a ninja star? So when he was shot, the only real error is that Stephon Clark wasn't carrying a basketball. Basketball bridges the gap. It makes the mysterious, threatening, volatile black man into something that we can all understand and root for. An athlete. No one would want to shoot an athlete. LeBron? Beloved. Stephen Curry? Beloved. Shaquille O Neal, star on the screen and on the court? Beloved. No one wants to shoot them. So, if every black man aged 15-45 carries a big, orange, Spalding basketball with them, I think we'd manage to cease the ire of police officers who are never racist, adequately trained, completely in the right and not in need of career change or public shaming and/or incarceration. But what about the other hand? Only takes one hand to hold a basketball constantly while in public. What if our idle hand raises suspicion from police? Solution is simple; two big orange basketballs. We all carry two basketballs with us. Or a basketball and basket of delicious Popeyes chicken? Perhaps a basketball in our left and a succulent watermelon in our right?

Yeah, that'll make us seem more human. That'll save us.

Simple.

The way I see it, Subway should pay me for this.

Fuck, alright, so I'm leaving my house to pick up my laundry and I'm walking down the street and this lady sees me walking towards her. When we get about a yard away, I see her tighten her grip, not on her purse, or shopping bags, but on her Subway sandwich bag.

I become livid.

Walking around as a black man I've received all sorts of suspicious, cautious, mildly racist looks. While profiling really hurts, and it is invariably wrong, it happens with such frequency I'm (nearly) used to it. But I usually see white women grab their purses tighter but never A FUCKING SUBWAY SANDWICH BAG.

Are you fucking daft lady?

Do you think niggas are really out here looking for 5 dollar footlongs? You're a fucking nut case if you think I give a fuck about your sandwich. Look at me, I'm wearing pants so tight they might as well be leggings and a shirt with a smiling hot dog on it, my shoes are Fred Perry and my glasses are Ray Bans. You think I'm plotting for your sandwich? Really? My outfit expensive as fuck, I pay for a service at the Laundromat that wash and folds my clothes for me. My peanut butter cost seventeen dollars, bitch, I don't care about your nasty ass sandwich. I'm fucking (primarily) Vegan. If I'm going to have a cheat day, it won't be for Subway, and it definitely won't be for a white person's subway. Y'all eat tuna sandwiches! Twelve inches of olive oil and tuna? You loony fucking weirdo.

The fuck I look like stealing a tuna sandwich! Idgaf about your sandwich, or you. Clutch your sandwich bag round me. I should clutch my culture/music/vocabulary around you, because that's what is really in danger of theft. Not your shitty fucking nine fucking grain, warm-ass tuna log.

You don't even have a drink and chips you broke bitch, fuck outta here.

Part 3

Deja once told me that she wished I was fuckboy.

But my fuck boy days are over. I'm now a fuck man. I will text you back in a timely fashion and I won't ghost you. But when I meet your family I'll talk shit about how your parents should have got divorced and how your brother is weak for the way he lets his kids talk to him. I'll be clear with my intentions and open honest dialogue about things that bother me. But I'll also try to opt out of date nights to play video games. I'll watch porn in the bathroom and then tell you I'm too distracted from my bad day at work to give you proper dick.

'But you can get on top though.'

A nice warm emptiness

Miranda, skinny as she was, always felt heavy it seemed to me. Not the sort of heaviness that comes with body weight,she ate regularly, or as regular as a girl trying not to gain weight can eat. Her self-image wasn't damaged by a shit-head parent/boyfriend or by the photograph of the emaciated/cartoonishly buxom models on Instagram. She was just very skinny and very pretty and thought about wizards and England and she liked music like mechanics like cars. And in this she was light, feather weighted.

But she felt heavy in her mind and in her breath and the nights she spent alone seemed to swallow her whole. Her awareness, her acute cognizance of the world and of people, and of how everything truly beautiful springs from pain weighed her down like an anchor on a ship. She moved dawdling in the night and although she had her cat (Bruno I think she told me, but it's been years, and I've known too many fucking cats with too many cute names to surely keep track of) and droves of potential suitors in DMs and at bars. She was so pretty that the patrons of any bar, from the men with the 4,000 dollar suits and Roth I.R.As in the Gold Coast to the busking crust punks in Bridgeport, couldn't help be started in that semi pathetic way men do.

Men salivated like coyotes when she was around, myself included, but I proudly admit a little less than the average hard leg. Miranda was legitimately a fine platonic companion and I'd seen what happened to the boys who ventured to transpose that line between platonic and romantic, I'd seen the husks she turned boys into.

I didn't want to be a husk, so I always kept it copasetic.

 Miranda was a melancholy sight at 3 am, disheveled and sometimes drunk and more than sometimes, cruel to people.

Her thoughts raced her off cliffs, nightly.

Seeing her at night sometimes was like realizing a clown looks less scary with make up on.

She called herself the "Unholy Ghost."

Every night the ghost would hold dominion over Miranda. She'd write in her journal, descriptive words but devoid of any spiritual importance thus lacking in artistic merit. She'd send me awful poetry.

She'd go on walks around the neighborhood but get nervous and run back to her apartment when the night denizens got too numbered and colored.

Then she'd hate herself for acting prejudice and pour more absinthe. She drank absinthe not because she liked the taste but because she felt less ashamed to be drinking alone if the drink was absinthe.

She'd listen to Mitski and Angel Olsen and cry. She never cried to male singers, she found them desperate and longing for pity and blowjobs. Which she knew personally, was the primary desires of the, male artist.

Her roommate was a girl named Alana who spent her nights dancing on the tops of bars or kissing men or thinking about kissing men or trying to be kissed by men or wanting to be on another planet. She was a normal girl in that sense. She looked like a model with her legs, thin and tanned, eyes departed and distant, slightly crooked teeth that made her lips pouty and archetypal of girls you don't see in real life.

Alana, the go-go dancer.

Miranda, the unholy ghost.

One night Alana brought home Randy, he was skinny but heavy like Miranda, but his unholy ghost was caged because he was trying to get between the holy legs of Alana.

And he did.

Randy banged Alana like a tambourine, and the sounds of their sex rattled Miranda like maracas.

The moans and smacks and slurps and low laughs and flickering of lighters for post coital cigarettes aggravated the unholy ghost. Miranda had never felt more alone then she did that night, hearing her roommate invite Randy to cum in her mouth.

Randy kept coming over. Alana liked him but not as much as she liked making Miranda sad. Alana thought Miranda was much prettier than she was, and if you asked 10 people,

I'd reckon 8 of them would agree. Alana thought Miranda was a melodramatic beauty who liked better music and had more interesting friends

Whenever they would talk at breakfast, Alana would always be a little amazed and confused and intimidated by Miranda's ideas and words. Whenever she used the bathroom after Miranda she couldn't smell a thing, even if Alana knew Miranda had just taken a shit.

"It's probably all that Whole Foods." Alan would say to her friends. "Health food makes your shit basically odorless. Right?"

One night, Randy came over to fuck Alana but she was too drunk and passed out so he talked to Miranda in the living room and they drank absinthe and rolled bad joints until they both lifted their heaviness and felt skinny and lithe. Randy wanted to kiss, and Miranda wanted to be banged like a tambourine, but they just talked until Alana woke up and to drink and smoke with them. Then Alana brought Randy into her room and blew him and they went to bed.

The next morning Randy pulled his normal vanishing act and Alana and Miranda talked about sex for the first time in the 6 months they'd lived together.

Alana was the expert, saying things callously and making pejorative yet correct statements:

"The asshole should be reserved for either your husband or someone rich."

But when Miranda said; "Sex is like drugs for both genders. For girls, it's like mushrooms, you plan it out beforehand, get yourself mentally and emotionally ready for the trip. For a guy, I think, it's like coke, after the first line goes, the second one is close behind then they wince and look all narcotized and then they try to score more." Alana was amazed and left for class feeling uncreative and unjustifiably slutty.

Randy came back because he forgot his cellphone charger and when he knocked Alana wasn't there and Miranda was getting out of the shower. She opened the door. After seeing Miranda with her wet hair and lily white shoulders exposed, Randy wanted to fuck and so did Miranda.

They made a knowing eye contact and then they kissed and Miranda whispered "I don't think you're that cute but you're all I think about recently."

Randy felt lucky and sad and guilty and then not guilty and he kissed Miranda with all he had.

Randy made love to her, and Miranda said "I need to be fucked." And she told me he did just that and that she squirted.

Women always say "squirted" with the giddiness of a child.

Alana never found out and they resigned their lease, but Miranda moved to New York so Alana had to scramble to find a sublet.

I see Alana out and we're cordial. She makes candles now, and has tattoos so I bet she feels interesting.

Miranda stopped sending me her poetry, and when I lived in New York she never responded to my invitation to hang out.

I wonder if the Unholy Ghost still walks her around at night.

I actually don't wonder, because I'm certain it does, and I don't know if she wanted to exorcise it.

Sometimes I'm not sure if I want to exorcise mine.

Ex-WHY-Zee

Ran into an ex last night two minutes before her date arrived to meet her.

What sort of cad doesn't show up early for a date to secure a seat and have a solo drink in silent, stoic preparation?

In those minutes, I rushed to her, not dissimilar to the way a dog does its master, and hugged her, and she said through an exasperated laugh that it'd been so long, it hadn't been that long, about nine months and there wasn't a week that went by where I haven't thought about how nice it would be to still have her around.

Our break up wasn't one of the amicable ones, it was blocked numbers and deleted social media accounts and the last time I called her I was in an airport in Louisiana in a ragged emotional state after a bachelor party that consisted 4 days of drinking literally enough to kill, or at least hospitalize some of you reading this.

 I had watched an episode of How I Met Your Mother in the Airbnb in New Orleans where Barney asks a woman for 30 minutes of her time and the soundtrack played and she said one day and even though it wasn't a set date it still gave Barney catharsis.

 I asked her for 30 minutes and she said no.

I asked about her cat, Bella, and she said Bella was none of my concern anymore.

She ended the conversation telling me she was blocking my number because hearing my voice made her miss me and if she missed me, she might have done something stupid.

I wanted her to do something stupid.

Her date was tall and had glasses but dressed like a nondescript, facsimile of every other black guy on a first date at this particular bar. No edge at all, he's name probably started with a D and he probably had a tattoo of a lion or Africa or something corny. At least he was black though, I couldn't stand losing her and Megan thee Stallion to the thin-lipped pink dicked horde in the same week.

I'd hope she would send him home early and sit next to me at the bar, for at least 30 minutes. I got so drunk that I didn't even notice her leave.

I met Brenda on a dating app and I was nearly certain she would be my last first date. (Even though that something white women in movies say.)

Or

I am a white woman in a movie.

I thought I loved a woman named Brenda who I met on Tinder. (My opening line was that she had the name of a lunch lady, and I feel it my responsibility to offer a caveat against using your formal introduction to someone, as an opportunity to career shame a fine and important vocation like the distribution of lunch. Whitney Houston told us in 1985 that the 'children are our future' and the future will certainly need sloppy joe and square cut pizza day. It is fine and noble work to dawn a hair net and to pick up the spatula.

Anyway back to Brenda,

She had tremendous skin and long legs and her own money. I liked the slow way she turned her head when I called her name, it was a satisfying build up to see her face, the way videos would load back in the dial up days of the internet. I loved the way she laughed, her eyes are squinted tight as if trying to sequester a fire exploding behind her eyelids. I loved that face so much I was compelled to put on long dumb shows of dance and odd voices to crack her up. I loved that face most of all.

I liked her long feminine fingers, a feature I like exponentially more seeing as though I had just wrapped up a fling with a woman with fingers like ten miniature hammerhead sharks. Imagine the grim aesthetics of receiving a hand job from a hand of vaguely phallic phalanges. (Insert your own Freud joke here.)

Brenda's hands looked French. I don't even know what that really means, but somehow I know exactly what it means and you do too.

 We hadn't been dating long, but the universe was made in six days and God rested on the seventh. Imagine if he had worked some over time how much better it would be. Maybe he would perfected the design on the platypus, added an extra layer of atmosphere, and reinforced the ice caps.

She was a catch, and I've never excelled in catching; I've always been a tad too nervous of my glasses being knocked off.

We hadn't been dating long but if binge watching 90 Day Fiancé taught me anything it's that time, with the right amalgamation of mental issues and familial pressure, when cultivating a relationship, is relative. We became mildly obsessed with each other.

We watched Wednesday date nights turn into 4 day staycations in our studio apartments where we'd bounce off each other like Newton's cradle, but sexier, and blacker.

Brenda once told me that sometimes my Chicago accent makes me sound like Tyresse and it was unbearably sexy. I sound like, R&B sensation and A-List actor Tyresse. He has a one-word name, something reserved for the sexiest people in the world like Bono, Seal, Rihanna, Madonna, or Bjork.

For Valentine's Day she bought us tickets to see Jeff Goldbloom's jazz band, and a remote control vibrator for me to use on her. It came with what at first glance appeared to be some sort of FitBit, a watch with several buttons that control speed and rhythm of the insert itself. Wearing it made me feel like a secret agent. Perverted James Bond.

The theater was laid out like an indoor amphitheater and an older, heavier woman with a slightly labored walk and a kind voice served us. I felt the slow creep of five or six screwdrivers fill me. Oranges are an excellent source of potassium which prevent cardiovascular disease, so screw drivers are literally good for the heart. And that is good for me because I don't have many interests these days, and some days I feel my heart has reached its maximum mileage limit, and no matter how far I go the odometer won't roll back.

It must have felt pretty insane to have something rattle like a hemi engine on your clit for the length of an entire Jazz concert doubling as a mid-life crisis pet project. Because that's what the Mildred Snitzer orchestra is. An old man's flight of fancy and excuse to get out of the house. I can only hope for a flight of fancy that is successful and lucrative. Jeff Goldbloom sauntered around the stage, noticeably drunk, lanky and long and speaking in that lush, meandering, staccato, stream of consciousness. After that he'd bang out a tune or two on his Steinway and then play drinking games with the audience.

It was hot for me because no one knew but us, and there is an innate sexiness in a secret, to be hidden, to have a sensation cloaked, to be erupting in a crowded room where no one is any ounce the wiser. Even the word cloak is very erotic.

Brenda was prone to intense bouts of vitriol though. And she'd never dated another black person and she make jokes about having to hope no one ever called her a 'nigger bitch' during sex, but I suspect she wanted that to actually happen, at least once, to see if it felt like she thought it would feel.

I'm not the fucking bunny slopes to date either. I come with a host of trust issues, stability questions, neurosis, Caligula levels of ego driven pettiness, plus I be snoring like a fucking character in a Hannah Barbara cartoon, and I'm a symbiotic-level big spoon. I'm on you hard and hot and breathing like Dodge Charger revving up. Like the fucking General Lee jumping a ramp. (Is there an official ramp count in the Dukes of Hazzard? Who was the urban planner for Hazard county, why were there so many ramps?)

Brenda told me that she didn't see a future because she didn't feel like I saw one, which is horseshit. She was the only face I saw when I looked ahead.

I can't blame anyone for peacing out on me. One time I made fun of some pants she was wearing, they were a fashion risk, not quite the mom jeans that are, inexplicably "in" right now, but they were so dorky and we were at a club and I told her I wouldn't dance with her as long as she had those pants on.

"I like my pants" she told me, her voice most always chipper yet, with those words, a somber glaze. I never saw her wear those pants again. And I'll always, if only mildly, be disgusted by that moment.

I know that a compliment from the right person can solidify any outfit choice. I was that person in your life, the person who was supposed to give her confidence about her pants, because, now, maybe through my guilt or past my ideas of what I wanted you to look like, I see those pants as my favorite pants she owned.

I should learn to just say 'I'm slowly resenting you, let's break up.'

Once my Ex and I were at a restaurant and on the TV they were playing Patlabor and I was excited because Patlabor is sweet and as far as anime goes, it's a pretty deep cut, you really gotta know your shit to even remember Patlabor. When the server noticed my enthusiasm while watching she remarked

"Oh, you like japanamation?" I nodded disgruntledly and when she walked away I told my girlfriend that only dorks and the elderly say japanamation. It's an anime, for Christ sakes. Just say anime. Then she went on a ten minute long assault on how I was so overly critical, and how could someone who doesn't know how to properly vacuum make fun of anyone, especially about something like anime. She goes on to tell me I'm on a high horse and I'm a bully. Then she starts crying and I'm looking at her like "You just ripped me a new blowhole, why the fuck are you crying?"

And as I look around I'm looking at people notice her cry and they're looking at me like I'm a fucking asshole, so I decide I'm not going to let her create this false reality so I want to start crying, so I start thinking about orphanages on Christmas, and the I'm like a Lawyer- Fallout Boy video, all sorts of sad shit to start crying that way I don't look so bad. At the end of the dinner I tip the server 20 dollars on a 31 dollar bill in order to apologize for my curt behavior and to appease my girlfriend, but she said 'Money wasn't the point'.

Later after we cooled down I thought about her 'money wasn't the point' retort, and since I habitually never know when to shut up, I thought about saying 'If money isn't the point I regret giving her that tip.' When I turned around to say she was grinning into her phone, I peaked over on the screen and it's a text from the same unsaved number she's been grinning at for weeks.

So I don't say it. Whatever I wanted from continuing the argument was already achieved.

Old

A woman asked me to "call her a car." I thought what a regal way to say you won't spend the night. Call me a car has that gleam of the upper crust, West Egg lifestyle Fitzgerald wrote about. She could have said 'order me an Uber nigga' or 'Its time for that Lyft now.'

But instead she said call me a car, and even though my bed was empty my spirit was full.

After she read my book my mom suggested for my second book I should talk more about 'the good stuff' So here goes;

or

Look for sheep.

One summer, I lived in the forest in New York my then girlfriend, the MAJOR ex-girlfriend, the one I thought I'd eventually grow grey with and have a litter of little Lawsons with. The important woman that, even with her discerning absence in my life, still teaches me lessons, still challenges me to be a better person.

We took our bosses car and set off to get tattoos in Connecticut. There were many issues with this trip.

1. We were on our way out of the relationship, we both knew it. We weren't officially together, but the forest brought the best out of us. Even though there were mountains of issues, sins that needed atonement, we still enjoyed each other that summer, more than we had in years.

2. We are two people who are prone to attacks of soul rendering anxiety. I'm a pretty anxious person, and the closer you circle in my orbit, the clearer the twine-thin strings that hold together my poise get. As bad as I was, she was worse, and for good reason. Things hadn't been easy for her, she lived a wild life with wild people, she ran the gamete of well-meaning but simultaneously toxic people, myself included.

3. Neither of us had a driver's license.

Here we were, broken up, anxious, and driving illegally while black in the serpentine roads of rural New York. We could have been arrested, imprisoned, our boss's car impounded, us invariably fired from our jobs, a slew of negative conditions could have followed, and we both knew this, but we did it anyway. We took the car and drove to another state to get tattoos. I wouldn't have done that with anyone else. It was fucking idiotic, impulsive, destructive behavior that can quickly change your life for the worse. But we did it together, because if I'm going to go down, I want to go down with my best friend.

The inside of the car was so steeped in nervousness that I was hyper aware of everything and I swear I felt my atoms vibrating. At one point she makes me pull over in a gas station to hyperventilate. Our GPS wasn't working and we made the one hour trip in a really rough two hours. She held my hand while I got my chest tattoo. On the way back she screamed so loud, I thought an 18 wheeler was careening towards us and was going to make us road kill, or that I'd missed a sign that read "No Road Ahead," and we were going to launch of a cliff and fucking blow up on the side of some craggy hill. But instead she screamed because on the passenger side window there was a farm, and on the farm there were hopping sheep, that I guess she thought were so cute that a shrill scream, not dissimilar to a woman being stabbed, was the only appropriate response. I laughed so hard, because my brain went to these morbid scenes of splayed out viscera and in reality it was just a couple dozen hopping sheep on a farm. She taught me, in that scream, that sometimes, even in moments of fear, even when you're worried, there are still things that make us so utterly happy that we scream. She didn't always see the sheep in situations, sometimes she saw the accident too, but that time she saw the hopping sheep and it challenged me to look for the sheep too.

A story about how I got exactly what I deserved.

It snowed. Hard and for four straight days. The news stations, fatalistic as they often are, coined the phrase "Snowpocalypse" to describe the conditions in Chicago during the winter of 2011. Around the city a photograph was circling about of an abandoned CTA bus on a snow covered stretch of Lake Shore Drive: the steering wheel festooned with ice stalagmites, seats dusted, if not completely swallowed whole by the snow. Through the windows of the bus, only a sprawling white, expanse existed. The bus took on the quality of a cave, like the city had been abandoned for hundreds of years and that the tech we had grown accustomed to shifted in purpose from the modern to the ancient, from the auxiliary to the base level. Like the bus no longer made sure humans got to work and instead it was a haven for artic wolves to keep their pups, for Frost Spiders to lay their eggs.

(I don't know what a Frost Spider is or why I was inclined to capitalize it but I have this feeling that if I don't they will descend upon me; The Frost Spiders)

The Snowpocalypse claimed 35 lives, mostly the homeless. Freezing to death is an archaic way die, especially when the bulk of humanity uses handheld super computers.

The Snowpocalypse cleared the streets of all life so the students at my college all had to huddle together in our apartments and dorms to fornicate and abuse drugs. Because rarely does weather deter liquor sales or lower vibrational impulses (especially mine). So as the semester came to end, it was paramount that you found some indoor company, because venturing out would prove fruitless. The zeitgeist would later coin this phenomenon 'cuffing season'. 'Weather based mating rituals of millennial' will be a class in at a liberal arts college in 100 years. Just kidding, college will probably be seen as obsolete in 50 years. Just in time for me to have fully re-paid my loans.

Gina was all the way in Atlanta, in film school.

 (I never told her this, but now seems like the right occasion; there is a film of hers I used to watch. It was about two women who realize they shouldn't be friends anymore and they have a friendship breakup at a diner. It was funny, like really funny. And I could pick out lines of dialogue her and I shared. It felt nice to finally be in her art since she populated mine so frequently.)

With my girlfriend 800 miles away and a wall of blizzard between us, I can't be blamed too explicitly for seeking to fill bed.

(This is of course bullshit and I realize I can and directly should in fact be blamed.)

The girl, this time, was Khloe but she went by Koko. Koko had thighs ample enough to crush a man skull and these deep dark eyes that when juxtaposed with her unyielding, perma-smile; made her look medicated. A Snowpoclaypse equates a man with strange bedfellows.

 Koko and I shacked up for about 3 weeks, the industry standard to ensure a coquetry doesn't become a tryst. I couldn't afford a tryst, or more honestly I didn't want to risk a tryst with Koko.

The Snowpocalypse had the bulk of flights canceled so in order to get to Chicago from Atlanta, Gina had to take a train. Which added twelve hours to her trip, giving me an entire extra day to philander with Koko.

This was undoubtedly a mistake; I flew too close to the sun on wings made of labial folds.

The night before Gina got back, Koko and myself had experienced some sort of domestic awkwardness: I'd drunk too much and threw up on her bedroom floor and was subsequently asked to leave. This was in the time before Uber revolutionized escaping awkwardness so we spent a painful 25 minutes trying multiple cab companies that were willing to drive from Pilsen to Wicker Park. I don't remember being remarkably regretful in the cab. Koko was fine and all, but she kissed with pursed lips, and I couldn't ever tell if she was doing it because she was mildly repulsed by me or if she was just a bad kisser. Plus she kicked me out for a simple, accidental transgression like puking on the floor, as if she didn't know I was a boundless pit. As if she didn't know that my first puke only meant a resurgence in energy was to come. My post-puke stroke game is a mighty force to contend with.

I made it to my apartment at around 1 AM. I'd like to lie and say I gargled mouthwash and showered in preparation for my girlfriend but that would be a lie and I refuse to lie in this go around.

Gina lied to her grandmother, a common practice, and said her bus didn't make it until a day after it actually did. She did this to maximize time with me. Her grandmother had a way of ushering her around, parading her to family and friends like the prized hog at the county fair. Although I understand Gina's grandmother. Gina was after all the heir to the McDonalds fortune, and Gina did after all have a drug problem.

Gina's at my door by noon. She always greeted me with the same voice. A voice lower and softer and breathier than the one she used with other people. It was like a sigh of relief, almost.

She wore a very nice knit cap with embroidery of a butterfly on it. Her hair was shorter now and sprinkled with snow at the curled ends. I was blasted by cold air when I opened the door so I rushed her inside but I wish I would have stood for a moment because the frozen hellscape juxtaposed her warmth perfectly. I hope that memory never fades. I hope when God plays back my miserable series of accidents that mold my life he lets me pause on that scene. Gina in her knit cap standing in front of white nothing. Warmth. Angelic warmth like the arbiter of salvation, standing there for me.

How I wish so deeply I would have stood a little longer, drank in the scene a little more. It was one of the last times I remember her happy to see me.

I usher her inside and after some talk and some looking into each other's eyes and a frozen pizza, we admit we are both tired. And we nap before I have to leave for my evening shift at the theater. It was Nutcracker season. An usher could make a lot of money during Nutcracker season; it wasn't uncommon for patrons to tip particularly friendly ushers, and with the influx of entire families patronizing the theater gave me the opportunity to charm the elderly right out of their social security.

I never locked my phone in those days, never password protected it. I wasn't the pentagon I thought, I didn't have secret launch codes or Area 51 schematics, my tech didn't need to be secret. With not-so-super power of hindsight I now realize not having a password to protect my secrets is so dumb especially for a boy who had so many secrets.

Secrets that took on names, names like Koko.

I woke up to the leading questions:

"What have you been doing this past week?" She's sitting up, back against the wall, long legs bent up, chin in her knees, one hand on her ankle.

"Nothing really," I say with confidence. In my warped head, I had done nothing, my drug consumption was at a low, I had finished my last semester of college, I was working a steady job and things between Koko and I were done.

"Are you sure?" she asks through a sigh. She nods as her gaze seems to chase unseen forces. I had learned that this was Gina's prelude to fury, and that I'd be the abject target of this fury. Her head turns toward me as I lay down, then her eyes follow:

"What type of name is Koko?" she asks as deep anguish turns her eyes glassy and focused. Koko's real name was Khloe but she didn't like to go by Khloe because it reminded her of her suburban upbringing and how it prompted within her all those bouts with being the 'black girl with the white name.' So when she moved to college she auditioned a new persona, the way we all seem to, and the one that stuck was Koko.

I'm telling you this, but to Gina I say:

"A close friend from school, she's going through a break up now." A drowsy prevarication.

"Oh, is she a close friend?" she asks with steadiness, the way cops read Miranda rights to crying perps.

"Yeah, she's cool, babe." The drowsiness is fading into anxiety, I think briefly of the trouble I'm in and also briefly about what time it could be, I need to go to work soon. If I could only ask to see my phone to check the time.

"Bhen is your close friend. And he's been waiting for a reply for two weeks. You like her more than Bhen? Or do you just want to fuck her?' She has me clocked.

"I don't..I fucking…" I mutter. I sit up and lean my back against the wall.

Gina starts to cry. I go in for a hug but I'm rebuffed.

"Don't fucking touch me. You're so fucking sloppy with everything. God…. God what am I doing here?" There is a sinking tragedy in that second 'God' that I can't forget either, and if hell is real, Beelzebub will make that my ringtone and will torture me with hearing it whenever student loan collection companies call for eternity.

That second God was so visceral I thought he'd answer. Gina had this way of speaking, measured, like she was reading from a script. Or maybe I was just so predictable.

She's crying when she finally tosses me my phone. I look at the messages to see a paragraph from Koko reporting how 'it was great getting to know me' and that 'I'm talented and cooler than most guys.' But how I had 'unchecked baggage and I couldn't ride her plane without checking it.' I thought about this line and wanted to compliment Koko on it. I check the time and it's 6:25, my shift at the theater is at 7:00 PM. If I leave now...

"Why do you do this shit to me?" Gina is breathing like a boxer in between rounds of a losing fight. Deep exhales through puckered lips.

I hate these moments because they last so long and ultimately mean nothing, and that's maybe the worst sentiment in this book of fucked up sentiments; these moments meant nothing because nothing had to change; she'd cry and cry and curse and maybe throw a punch or a glass.

But ultimately nothing would change. She would take me back and the cycle would continue, the wheel would turn, every spoke intact. We were black Sid and Nancy, we were together, indefinitely, and there was nothing else.

With this in mind, I get up and leave the bed.

"What the fuck are doing?" Gina asks, the sadness seemingly dissolved into a steam of agitation.

"I have work babe I can't….Not right now, look stay here, we will talk about everything ok?" This job was the one thing that tethered me to adulthood, the one healthy practice I had. It didn't really pay bills, my parents did that. It did however spare me, in small degrees, from feeling completely derelict. My job, my mandated bowtie and my name tag and my bi-weekly 160 dollar paychecks, it was the one and only thing that made me feel like any forward progression was occurring on my end.

She saw this version of me, this small, post-college, lost version and she loved it like she loved me at my absolute worst. The audacity I had to ignore such a love.

I begin to get ready and a volley of curses are thrown my way.

"How the fuck can you seriously even think about leaving right now, Adam?" She garbles through desperation.

"I have to go to work, I need a job don't I?"

"But what the fuck, right now, are you seriously about to leave?"

"I have too, I'm sorry I don't know what, I don't know what I can do." I pause every now and then to look at her, she's sitting on the bed, shaking her head and looking at me in disbelief.

We were each other's best friends in the classic childhood sense. Imagine our spirits as two children on a swingset on a hill overlooking a city as the sun sets. Not even holding hands, we didn't need to touch to be tethered.

I'd met her in the hallway of her dorm room, she was on the phone, her roommate slept inside, and Gina, always conscientious , spoke outside so as to not wake her. I saw her with her hair down to her waist and her legs and her ass and her smile and I asked her when she'd be done with her phone call, she shot me a smile and an index finger, she heads into her room, a few moments pass then she emerges, phoneless.

I don't know what we talked about, but it was a Rube Goldberg machine, one sentence led to another and it seemed far fetched and unattainable but it was intricate and beautiful and done by divine design. It was a perfect storm. And I think we both felt it in that moment. And it wasn't love at first sight, that's dumb notion for concocted to sell make up and movie tickets. Instead it was like the teeth of a great and giant zipper, binding together. It was like finding the missing mate to sock you were content with wearing forever mix-matched.

I'd trade 10 years of my life to sit in that hallway one more night. I'd die at 50 if it meant I could feel that once more.

I knew and I loved everything about her. She only ate Stephen Colbert ice cream flavor, Ameri-cone dream. After Gina, I stopped learning girl's last names, dietary restrictions, and favorite colors.

I was her best friend, and I was abandoning her for a shift at the theater where I made $9.25 an hour.

After I'm dressed, still thoroughly unshowered, a mere swabbing of deodorant to stabilize me in whatever sub-par hygiene state I was, I move from the bedroom to the living room, where my boots and coat are stationed.

"Adam, you cannot go anywhere, I'm…. If you go we're done."

"Ok, let it be done. I need to go."

"That's what you want?"

"No, not at all, I want to talk to you and be with you and love you but you're the one giving ultimatums." Ultimatums was a toxic-relationship buzzword back then. I wielded the word 'ultimatum' like Thor's hammer. I'd fuck up, refuse to talk, she'd threaten to leave, I'd say 'Oh you're presenting an ultimatum.' And she'd somehow get buried under the guilt of being anything other than right and good and true and she'd concede.

This time felt different. Maybe it was cold. If you believe a certain Potawatomi native tribe, every snowflake is the spirit of an ancestor, maybe the snow spoke to her. Someone needed to in those days.

"I swear to God, Adam." Her eyes are like fucking lasers. Which is particularly scary because she smiled even in her sleep sometimes. Gina was nearly always a portrait of a chipper. Even the nights she got so fucked up she wobbled like a baby bird. Even with those marks up and down her arms that looked like white ladder rungs. She was always smiling unless she was dealing with me.

This plays out for a few more minutes and as I get on my coat and boots and place my shiny black work shoes in my backpack she pleads with me.

Pleading with me, even though I'm the fucking asshole.

Before long I'm on the train to work; that's when the texting starts.

(I developed an almost singeing pain when I received multiple text messages from the same person. I launch myself into a frenzied panic. The notification jingle becomes gong strikes, it's like I develop some sort of hyperacusis due to trauma. And I think I can trace it back to Gina's string of texts to me that day.)

It was one of those moments where your soul leaves your body and you're able to view yourself from the vantage point of a floating third party, as if watching yourself on film.

What did "sorry for your laptop" mean?

It was perfect, it was fucking art. The way she lured me into the right hook that was her revelation. Her revelation that I am and will never be fit to touch.

"I'm sorry too. I'm also sorry for your clothes. And your room. And your laptop." I was stuck. The confusion of her words built into a sudden salvo of revelation. Yet still, there was a muddled sense of terror. I couldn't be that terrified. I had work. I had to take tickets and lead old women to seats and make sure kids didn't kick the backs of chairs. I had to make sure Big Nick had a smoke break buddy. (He was paranoid of being the only black person on any street at any given time, so when he went for his smoke breaks, he needed another black usher to come with him. Something about 'They be abducting niggas.') I had to conduct a life without knowing the condition of my stuff.

The theater opened and hundreds of children, with hundred parents came trampling in. The lobby of an internationally known theater during Nutcracker season is always an incredible sight. It's like Grand Central Station but with champagne flutes and better coats. The two biggest sellers at the concession stand are popcorn and wine, both of which are highly addictive and easily spilled.

I spend the first hour of my shift with a broom and dustpan sweeping popcorn. Big Nick notices I'm 'off.'

"You good bro?" Big Nick says, but at a distance and with a grimace, the way you'd ask someone who you suspected was about to vomit.

 "I feel like a ghost," I say; I'm prone to responses nebulous and vague. Beyond 'prone' even, maybe overly fond of.

"Yeah man you seem like it. Your lady's in town right?"

"Yeah she is.."

"And y'all, are having…" He pauses. "The best time ever it looks like."

"Nah man, we aren't. Having to be at fucking work with shit, heavy shit on your mind is like.."

"Watching a crocodile eat a baby then having to sell car insurance. You're mind ain't really on the rate for collision coverage on a Mazda."

I idly sweep nothing into the dust pan before I look up and say "That, was really fucking accurate, Nick."

The walk back to my house from the train station seemed slow due to a combination of weather, light, and will. It was a trudge, if there has ever been one. Part of me had believed there was a chance she was bluffing, that maybe it was all a ploy to cause me maximum discomfort, to get my mind racing to worse. Maybe it was the shitty boyfriend's version of scared straight; but this would not have scared me straight. I did in fact need what it was it was she had given me.

I opened my door to see a hellscape of glass, detergent splattered all over the walls, settined (?) in permanently stained, my window left open letting blades of air and snow in. When I walk over the mounds of clothes stripped from my wardrobe, doused in what I thought was wine, which she has since clarified to me as being baptized in toilet water, to close my window, I see a frosty white hill beneath, a sleeve poking out, I recognize the plaid pattern, it is a red shirt I have worn, I make out another color pattern from beneath the small frosty hill, my flamingo polo. It quickly registers that the entire snow-capped mesa is made of clothes Gina has thrown out of the window of our second story apartment.

Cooper hears me open the door and bolts out of his bedroom down the hall sporting a truly cunty smirk. He tells me he saw the whole fantastic thing:

Gina is drinking red wine with her headphones in smoking a cigarette smashing light bulbs on my floor, face damp and blackened from tears and eyeliner, she stood on my bed with snow heavy boots and cried as she ripped up shirts and books. Cooper said she wore her headphones and they were blasting so loud she hadn't heard him open the door.

"She rain danced on your fucking laptop man," he says through a smile

I ask him why didn't he text me to let me know, he says he didn't know what to say but I know that Cooper is a fucking twerp and he wanted to witness the dismay on my face.

Cooper was my age but got a fake ID that changed his name to Franco so he could pretend to be James Franco's cousin. What's worse is that it would work, and girls would come over and I'd have to corroborate, as if lying to my own girlfriend wasn't morally degrading enough already.

"Fuck. This…She." I say looking down at my clothes and my room and my walls - my signed Ville Valo poster ripped down the middle, two impudent flaps of paper adorned my wall, like the errant ears of a faceless man.

I feel my heart plummet down a trap door but not to its death. Plummet down to a significantly difficult and arduous climb up. And I'm sure we all can relate to the notion that sometimes a swift death can sound more appealing than a tumultuous rehabilitation. Sometimes we only have the strength to call it quits.

My laptop was flattened and splintered. I'd later find out that she gave it some American History X curb stomps, like she had taught a Clydesdale how to count to ten. It was flat like a Hannah-Barbera character after an anvil drops on it.

I spent the remaining hours of that night ensuring that at the very least the glass was up. And let me tell you finding a needle in a haystack has a higher success rate then rummaging through a pile of soggy clothes for glass. It was a night of toil and sadness and what compounded that sadness was the thought that somewhere Gina was either completely fine or completely wrecked and I was the cause.

Or perhaps she was completely naked. We broke up for a week in college and she spared no time in rushing into the sack with a guy who looked like a Jonas Brother with polio. I shudder to think who her post destruction partner could have been.

I don't know any other form of torture worse than assuming the condition of a love one. In all manners of duress or undress. Another man, two more men, a woman, how the fuck could I complete with a woman?

I slept on the couch that night, and a few more after that.

Most mornings after were spent wallowing in a crust of my own guilt. It was difficult to do much of anything, including the essential tasks that human life requires: eating and sleeping and bathing etc.

Everything felt like labor, everything felt like an obligation to a family member you don't really know, everything felt like sitting through traffic with a headache; miserable.

Heartache is like a wart on your nose, always in your line of sight, ever present in most states of consciousness. With a wart on your nose people will still talk to you and laugh at your jokes but then you'll remind yourself of the wart and fixate and all of a sudden the world will seem to deflate and you'll be less funny and more ghastly.

Eventually Nancy called to tell me about the strange etching on the front of the building.

Nancy was our land lady from Vietnam and by all estimation she had to be in her early 300s. Tiny and moving with a slow shuffle; her English was as broken as a drunk girl named Miranda's iPhone screen on her 21st birthday. More broken than a Seether song featuring Evanescence. One time I called her to send a repairman to fix a hole in a wall, no repairman showed, instead Nancy came, with a caulk gun and a step ladder. She proceeded to climb the ladder, in her shaky, elderly, worrisome manner, she takes an hour, an incredibly tense hour. If she were to fall her ghost would haunt us. Hollowing in shattered English about how the rent was late.

This is not meant to sound ageist, there are a great many senior citizens who are capable of physical feats I couldn't dream of. There are spry, active, limber older people who can perform cartwheels and walk slacklines. Nancy was not one of these elders. Nancy moved a little slower than Frankenstein, and Frankenstein was a reanimated cadaver made from the 1800s.

"You have a bad friend," Nancy utters through the phone.

"I'm sorry?" I say into the phone, trying to piece together her words. People with accents never seem to be that cognizant of their accents, the undulation of speed and volume never quite acknowledging the fact that the listener may have no fucking clue what they are saying. But yet and still Nancy's English is leaps and bounds better than my Vietnamese, so there's that.

"You have a bad friend." She laughs, I think.

"I'm sorry Nancy, I'm not sure what you mean." I have tons of bad friends but what the hell does she know about any of them.

"You need to clean. Must wash brick."

"Bricks. Yes bricks." I give up trying to decipher her coded message and default to agreeing. Agreeing is the fastest way to get someone to shut up.

After the phone call ends I spend a few moments on the couch mulling over what exactly Nancy was trying to tell me. Was she going senile? Was she speaking in code? Did she mean a brick of cocaine? Was 'bad friend' an acronym for something?

Later I leave the couch to get Italian Beef and on my way back I see the Letters, etched in crimson lipstick. "Adam, I fucking hope she was worth it." On the front of my apartment building.

I stared at it for around 3 minutes, my Italian beef getting cold in the sub-zero winds. I stared without blinking, thinking soft thoughts, or thoughts that hit me softly. Thoughts like:

Is this real?

How long has this been here?

How many people have taken pictures of this?

I started with admiration too. The angles, the scrawl, the artful calligraphy of it all. Banksy would have had to nod in approval. The spirit of Keith Haring guided her. Basquiat piloted her hands, clean strokes, like she'd trained for.

The graffiti wasn't here yesterday, I went to work yesterday. This had to have happened today, she'd plotted this, she came back, maybe in the dead of night, maybe an hour ago, she was here and did this. I started with silent, soft veneration. She really was the woman of my dreams and this act, criminal and scornful and bitter as it was; to me I saw a sweeping holistic testament to passion. The artistry in every stroke, the angles that met to form the A in my name.

Van Gogh eats your ear off.

I spent the afternoon on the phone, asking about graffiti removal services, a process you have to go through the police for. I spent an hour on wait lists and with operators after calling secondary numbers only for them to tell that the service is only available to certain zip codes for businesses.

I find the number of a company and they laugh when I tell them what is written. They say the city can give me a fine if it's on the building too long, due to the profanity. They offer to clean it for $300. I have $43.83. $300.00 literally took two months to raise in that time.

I wanted to call her to get rid of it, she was rich for fucksake. Her grandmother lived in the same building as Luol Deng, She had a fucking Black Card and once we went to Victoria Secrets and she racked up a $400 tab.

"I hate doing stuff like this," she said, insisting she hold the bags. Like the purchases were her burden. She was so cool in that way, all the resources and none of the proclivity for the frivolous. She treated spending money like a burden, unless it was on booze, drugs, or food.

But I couldn't call her, I was happy she was gone, gone away from me so I couldn't hurt her any longer, I'm happy she'd destroyed stuff because then maybe, we could be even, and the karmic debt I owed for three years of benign torture could be squared away, and maybe I'd be free to court (torture) another woman.

So I didn't call her and in the meanwhile I started selling weed to get the money for a new laptop and clothes and the graffiti removal service. I got a front on a quad and sent a mass text to everyone in my phone that I was the new weed man on campus. Making home deliveries in the Snowpocalypse was lucrative, I'd meet kids outside of dorms and at Panera Bread. Panera means bread in Spanish so to bilingual people the restaurant is called 'Bread Bread.'

I was all around the city with a backpack full of weed, a heart bruised, and a nose running like it was following the fucking North Star to freedom. The winter air was thin like a bat's wing and all the kids would invite me to smoke a bowl with them before I went back out in the cold, and I would, and I'd smoke, and just get more depressed and there was a paroxysm I'd feel whenever my phone would ring and it wasn't Gina, just the same hollow interaction: one asshole pothead telling me they got my number from another wastoid pothead seeing if I could hook up a sale.

I made about $150 a week, minus the re-up cost of $90 plus, I saw a $60 profit, transportation was free because I was still on the last six months of a student CTA pass that gave me free rides all over town.

I'd make these late trips, on buses I knew nothing about. The city lives on buses and trains and at night, that's the blood of Chicago, the most living area. It was negative 12 and it was 1 AM and the 72 bus had a palpable pulse, a couple with shopping bags, a man who seemed to laugh at his own reflection in the window of the bus. A woman who was oscillating between sleeping and silently weeping. Me, with a backpack full of weed, three different strands that I make up my own sales pitch for.

"Dude I smoke weed but this Blueberry Starship is something serious."

One of my favorites was when a kid would ask me about insert generic weed name here and I'd say something caustic and vaguely threatening like:

"To be real bro, I'd stay away from this one, like, for real." And I'd watch the Cheshire cat-like smile grow on the faces of the young and stoned and I knew I'd make a bigger sale and in most cases I'd get a text saying "Bro you were right me and my friend are still baked. I'll definitely hit you up."

I sold weed until February when the Snow Apocalypse had broken and rolled back, giving way to just a plain, run of the mill, miserably cold Chicago February. I used the weed money for a mac-book, I also bought Guild Wars 2 and joined a role-play server where I had three in-character relationships. (I was a handsome, 6'3 illusionist Mesmer with emo hair and a pencil mustache and I had the 'bow' emote hot keyed so whenever I met a female character I was only a shift-key 7 from dazzling her.)

I listened to a lot of Black Sabbath during the month we were apart. So many people think of Black Sabbath has satanic imagery, occult worship, or they equate it to Ozzy's exploits. Snorting lines of fire ants and biting heads off bats. Or worse they see a t-shirt in a Target and want to wear the aesthetic and I guess that's cool if it puts money in the band's pocket. But Sabbath had more blues and ballads than its heavy metal classifications would lead one to believe. A lot of the lyrics are of blue-collar trials mixed with fantasy. It's like if Aretha Franklin took acid and went to Comic Con.

All the while I knew Gina was somewhere either caring deeply or not at all. Chicago thawed out, we'd missed Christmas and New Years, my parents asked about her, my Dad the most. But he asked with a tone that signified he knew she was gone, but he asked anyway, vehemently, fiendishly.

Or maybe he wanted his son to open up and tell his old man about how he'd lost the woman that was supposed to be the finished line.

You see my dad keeps a clipping of a date in January on his cork board at home, it's the weekend of my dad's birthday in 2011. My dad, my mom, Gina and me met at a west loop Michelin rated restaurant that posed like a roadside diner, because that's what the rich like; the suspension of disbelief. How else could they get away with being incredulous like the rest of us. We drank milkshakes with bourbon in them, we laughed and talked and while my dad says he's proud of me often, I think this time he actually was. He had a reason to, you see cohesive partnerships are feats, much akin to climbing mountains or running with the bulls. In fact maybe more difficult; imagine how many mountain climbers can't even get second dates.

Finding a beautiful partner who feeds your soul and makes you happy is like finding a needle in a bucket of acid. Gina made the world envious she was all legs that stretched tall enough to scrape God's ball sack, the dainty way she walked, it was dainty in defiance of her height and her ass. And her ass was a powerful sight, like something out of a Ying Yang Twins video, and to think that would grow out of the thighs of a woman who wrote a dissertation on Yorgos Lanthimos films.

It was my wet dream. Because I'm a pseudo-intellectual and a pervert. (There has been no more clear description of me to ever exist.)

I was scared almost the entire time Gina was gone. It felt similar to that plunging feeling I'd get as a kid when I realized my memory card had an error and all my saved data, the 50 hours of Final Fantasy, the entirety of my Monster Rancher Bestiary, was gone, all my work, my fanatic devotion, erased and nothing that even resembled a spec of hope to get it back.

And even now as I write with 30 year old fingers; having seen the effects of dementia and addiction and depression and schizophrenia. Having seen wanton despair in the faces of children (I'm a teacher and pubescent despair is the house special.) and in the faces of the homeless. There is still nothing I fear as deeply, no sensation I feel so dreadfully and slicing in between my solar plexus like a spike through the heart, like that of being helpless as someone walks out the door. The desperate panic, the quickened breathing, the lightning bolts of glimpses into a solitary future. Nothing binds to my bones more than a breakup I don't want. I guess I'm still a romantic.

I think when you're in a relationship it's like inviting someone into your house through one central door. And the goal, if you love the person or like them or just want them to stay around, is to minimize other exits. You want to supply for the person inside your house whatever they desire, but without ever opening the door. But I think in relationships we build auxiliary exits, these exits are constructed by opinions; on food or politics or religion or child care. These exits are built by disagreements and apologies, they are built by boundaries being crossed. These exits are built by others, taller, better jobs, softer hands, and better hair. They are built by shame and guilt and neurosis and our parents. And sometimes you don't know why they are built, you just know it's the exit they took when they left.

And you try to board up the exits, you work out, you attend church with them, you remember their favorite candy and surprise them with it on their pillow case. You fold their laundry, you don't stay out too late with your coworkers, you invite them places, and some of the exits get cemented over or boarded up, but all it takes is one exit for them to leave, all they need is one door and the proper inclination and all the wood and brick is for shit.

Eventually I had to sleep in my bed because Cooper was being a pain and said that I paid rent for a bedroom and sleeping on the couch in a common area for a week was 'inconsiderate' or something fucking dweeby like that.

Fucking.

Loser.

That night I lay in bed and thought about how Gina and I went, took Molly and went on a boat cruise. We ate and after diner we found a quiet place to mumble and stroke one another's faces, under the stars, I don't remember a single fucking face other hers, we might has well had been alone in the dining room, on that boat, in the universe.

Another night we decided to make it a point to spend the hour that vanishes when Daylight savings time comes with just each other, it was our lost hour, we talked about how bartenders and strippers account for this hour. We thought about the idea of manipulating time, we found that one of the reasons Daylight Saving time was still in effect was the idea that it bolstered the economy, people shopped more and spent more money when the sun was up.

One summer we lived in the forest in New York. We took our bosses car and set off to get tattoos in Connecticut. Neither of them had a driver's license and this was a source of intense elation and anxiety. We are both two people who are prone to attacks of soul rending anxiety. I'm a pretty anxious person, and the closer you circle in my orbit, the clearer the twine thin strings that hold together my posie get, and Gina had seen it all. And as bad as I was, she was worse, and for good reason. Things hadn't been easy for her, she lived a wild life with wild people, she ran the gamete of well-meaning but simultaneously toxic people, myself included.

We could have been arrested, imprisoned, our boss's car impounded, us invariably fired from our jobs, a slew of miniature calamities could have followed, and we both knew this, but we did it anyway, we took the car and drove to another state to get tattoos. I wouldn't have did that with anyone else, it was idiotic, it was impulsive, it was destructive behavior that can alter ones life for the worse. But we did it together, because we were going to go down, it had to be with each other, it had to be with our best friend. The inside of the car was so steeped in nervousness that I swear I feel my atoms vibrating. At one point she makes me pull over in a gas station to hyperventilate. Once we were about 15 minutes away from our destination she screamed so loud, I thought an 18 wheeler was careening towards us and was going to make us road kill, or that I'd missed a sign that read 'No Road Ahead.' and we were going to launch of a cliff and fucking blow up on the side of some craggy hill. But instead she screamed because on the passenger side window there was a farm, and on the farm there were hopping sheep, that I guess she thought were so cute, that a shrill, scream, not dissimilar to a woman being stabbed, was the only appropriate response. I laughed so hard, because I went to these morbid scenes of splayed out viscera and in reality it was just a couple dozen hopping sheep on a farm. She taught me, in that scream, that sometimes, even in moments of fear, even when you're worried, there are still things that make us so utterly happy that we scream. She didn't always see the sheep in situations, sometimes she saw the accident too, but that time she saw the hopping sheep and it challenged me to look for the sheep too.

Eventually Gina comes back, and we make up, or as made up as co-dependent lovers in their early 20s can be.

It was a great 2 week, save for the Snowpocaplyse that had given Gina a cold I was certainly not certified to treat.

She had this hack, she sounded like General Grievous from Star Wars. Her temperature was so high and it amazed me that skin could get that hot, she felt like she'd be in a toaster oven, but not long enough to fully heat. This was before UberEats, and maybe in the infancy of Grubhub, I walked to the Thai-Fusion restaurant to get soup.

 Or rather once I did, I'm such a bad boyfriend.

Once during one of her fever naps where she garbled and snored in such a boorish way it was nearly adorable; I looked at her MacBook's photos; In her MacBook were pictures of her and her man who she's still with today. In one he was grabbing her ass like it was basketball and he was taking it to the hole. I wasn't jealous, I was happy, because Gina was my friend, and she deserved happiness.

Gina was my best friend, we'd watch movies and eat together and trade opinions and stories and mannerisms. We became these mirror images of one another, we lived in choreography. She became imprinted on me, that's what friends do, that's the ultimate nature of friendship, I think.

I don't know how to make friends, and I think that comes from a memory I have of my childhood; I'm 5 years old and I'm in my parents' bedroom on the second floor, outside of my house, Dexter and Dallas, the twin grandchildren of my elderly neighbor Ms. Burnett are outside of my house on bikes, I hear them from Texas who visited;

"We don't want to be your friend anymore."

"Why?"

"We heard what you said?"

"What did I say?"

"Don't lie, we heard what you said and we aren't your friend anymore."

I remember being hurt but not moved to tears, I sat on the floor, and wondered for a little bit, I heard them say 'we can still see you.' As if I was watching, hidden from the window, and I wasn't, I had resigned, Martin had won, sniveling Martin had won and I never saw Dexter and Dallas again, maybe they'd come to visit Chicago some summers but stayed inside.

Ever since then my willingness to let people in had been less than frequent. I fancied myself a Ferris wheel operator. Because a Ferris Wheel operator sees everyone as they turn, all the faces, transient and travelling, and while the Ferris Wheel Operator has the power to speed up the ride or stop the ride so that the people in the highest cart can share the view with birds, ultimately the ride stops, and the riders get off and give way to another set and Ferris Wheel Operator pushes the lever and the ride starts again.

And the riders laugh and take photos and contemplate the intricacies of the human condition, but the Operator stays stationary, on the ground, levering hard, still but in control.

We'd been together 4 years, but time isn't a healthy metric when it comes to ground beef and love. 'Stick it out.' Is an unhelpful ultimately unhealthy expression.

If Elon Musk is right and life as we know it is a simulation created by a celestial being, and the simulation crashed and the being said he only had could only reboot 2 other people I'd have chosen Gina twice. We could have lived in the ghost world, subsisting wholly on non-perishables and each other. What a fine time the three of us could have had, from now until the end of us. Do clones die at the same time? And that's what I think love is, letting everyone else stay dead so you and your special person can enjoy a life of no lines.

In her macbook were pictures of her and her man who she's still with today.

We talked about it.

"If you didn't care you wouldn't have gone through my pictures in the first place." She said, her eyes with a different desperation.

"I looked because…"

"Ha-Ha Ha you care, you care and you don't want to." Gina sing-songs to cut me off. I never got what that meant until I started writing this, she'd destroyed my room because she cared so deeply, and here I was, joking about the other man, that must have seemed like I really didn't care.

That must have made Gina feel like her actions were truly out of proportion.

So maybe that's why I wrote this, to retract the notion that I wasn't angry because I didn't care, I wasn't angry because I knew she deserved happiness.